ADVANCED SPA

Unlocking the Full Potential of NLP in Python

BENJAMIN SAMUEL

TABLE OF CONTENT

PREFACE

Welcome to the world of spaCy, a library that has redefined how we approach Natural Language Processing (NLP) in Python. In an age where text data is ubiquitous – from sprawling social media feeds to intricate scientific publications – the ability to understand, analyze, and extract meaningful insights from language has become paramount. Whether you're a seasoned data scientist, a curious developer, or an enthusiastic newcomer to the field, spaCy offers an elegant, efficient, and powerful toolkit to navigate this linguistic landscape.

This book is your comprehensive guide to harnessing the full potential of spaCy. We embark on a journey that starts with the fundamental building blocks of text processing and progressively delves into advanced techniques for building sophisticated NLP pipelines. You'll discover how spaCy's intuitive API and carefully designed architecture streamline complex tasks, allowing you to focus on extracting value from your data rather than wrestling with intricate implementation details.

More than just a technical manual, this book aims to provide a practical understanding of NLP concepts through the lens of spaCy. We'll explore core tasks like tokenization, part-of-speech tagging, named entity recognition, and dependency parsing, illustrating how spaCy's pre-trained models and customizable components can be leveraged for real-world applications.

As we progress, we'll venture into more advanced territories, including training custom models for specific domains, extracting complex information structures, and even deploying your NLP solutions as robust and scalable services. We'll also touch upon the exciting possibilities of integrating cutting-edge transformer models within the spaCy ecosystem, unlocking new levels of accuracy and understanding.

This book is written with the belief that learning should be both informative and engaging. You'll find clear explanations, practical code examples, and insights into the underlying principles that drive spaCy's effectiveness. By the end of this journey, you'll not only be proficient in using spaCy but also equipped with the knowledge to tackle a wide array of NLP challenges with confidence and creativity.

So, whether you're looking to build intelligent chatbots, analyze vast quantities of text data, extract key information from documents, or explore the fascinating intersection of language and artificial intelligence, let spaCy be your guide. Prepare to unlock the power hidden within words and discover the transformative potential of Natural Language Processing. Let's begin.

CHAPTER 1

Architecting Scalable NLP Pipelines with spaCy

1.1 Designing for High-Throughput Text Processing

Designing for high-throughput text processing with spaCy involves architecting your NLP pipelines to handle a large volume of text data efficiently. This requires careful consideration of various factors, from how you load and process data to the components you use and how you optimize their execution.

One key aspect is **efficient data loading and batching**. Instead of processing documents one by one, spaCy excels when you feed it iterators of text. This allows spaCy to manage its internal data structures more effectively.

Python

```python
import spacy

nlp = spacy.load("en_core_web_sm")

def get_large_text_corpus(file_path):
    with open(file_path, 'r', encoding='utf-8') as f:
        for line in f:
            yield line.strip()

texts = get_large_text_corpus("large_text_file.txt")
docs = nlp.pipe(texts, batch_size=1000, n_process=4) # Process
in batches and in parallel
```

```
for doc in docs:
    # Process each document
    print(doc.text[:50])
```

In this example, `nlp.pipe` is crucial. It processes texts in batches (here, 1000 at a time), which significantly reduces the overhead of Python function calls for each document. The `n_process` argument enables parallel processing across multiple CPU cores, further boosting throughput. **Choosing an appropriate** `batch_size` **and** `n_process` often involves experimentation based on your hardware and the complexity of your pipeline.

Another consideration is **selecting the right spaCy components**. Not all components are necessary for every task. If you only need named entities, you can disable other pipeline stages to save processing time and memory:

Python

```
nlp_ner = spacy.load("en_core_web_sm", disable=["tok2vec", "tagger", "parser", "attribute_ruler", "lemmatizer"])

texts = ["Apple is looking at buying U.K. startup for $1 billion", "Google announced a new AI model."]
docs = nlp_ner.pipe(texts)
for doc in docs:
    print(doc.ents)
```

Here, we explicitly disable components we don't need, making the processing faster and lighter. For high-throughput scenarios, **customizing your pipeline** to include only essential components is vital.

Furthermore, **leveraging spaCy's data structures efficiently** contributes to performance. The Doc object is designed for efficient access to linguistic annotations. Avoid redundant computations or conversions within your processing loop. Once a Doc object is created, you can access various attributes like tokens, entities, and their properties directly.

Finally, consider **hardware acceleration** if your workload demands it. Libraries like cupy can be integrated with spaCy for GPU-based processing, especially beneficial when using larger transformer models.

In summary, designing for high-throughput text processing with spaCy involves:

Efficient data loading and batch processing using `nlp.pipe`.

Strategic selection and disabling of unnecessary pipeline components.

Optimal choice of `batch_size` **and** `n_process` **for parallel processing**.

Efficiently utilizing spaCy's Doc **object and its attributes**.

Exploring hardware acceleration with libraries like cupy **when applicable**.

1.2 Leveraging spaCy's Components for Custom Pipelines

Leveraging spaCy's components for custom pipelines is a powerful way to tailor your NLP workflows to specific needs. spaCy's architecture is built around a series of modular components that process the `Doc` object in a defined order. You can rearrange these components, remove default ones, and add your own custom components to achieve specialized functionalities.

The `nlp.pipeline` attribute gives you a list of the currently active components and their names in the order they are executed:

Python

```
import spacy

nlp = spacy.load("en_core_web_sm")
print(nlp.pipeline)
```

This will typically output something like `[('tok2vec', <spacy.pipeline.tok2vec.Tok2Vec>), ('tagger', <spacy.pipeline.tagger.Tagger>), ('parser', <spacy.pipeline.dep_parser.DependencyParser>), ('attribute_ruler', <spacy.pipeline.attributeruler.AttributeRuler>), ('lemmatizer', <spacy.lang.en.lemmatizer.Lemmatizer>), ('ner', <spacy.pipeline.ner.EntityRecognizer>)]`.

To create a custom pipeline, you can load a base model and then modify its components. For instance, if you only need tokenization and a custom entity recognizer, you can remove the default NER component and add your own:

Python

```
import spacy

nlp = spacy.load("en_core_web_sm")
```

```python
# Remove the default NER component
nlp.remove_pipe("ner")

# Define a custom component (for demonstration, it does nothing)
def custom_entity_recognizer(doc):
    doc.ents = [] # Your custom logic to identify entities would go here
    return doc

# Add the custom component to the pipeline
nlp.add_pipe(custom_entity_recognizer, name="custom_ner")

print(nlp.pipeline)

doc = nlp("This is some text about a company called Acme Corp.")
print(doc.ents) # Will be empty as our custom component doesn't identify entities
```

The `nlp.add_pipe()` method allows you to insert your custom component at a specific position in the pipeline using the `before`, `after`, or `first/last` arguments. The `name` argument is crucial for referencing and managing your components.

Custom components are typically functions that take a `Doc` object as input and return the modified `Doc` object. They can perform various tasks, such as:

Adding custom linguistic annotations: Identifying specific patterns or applying rule-based logic.

Integrating external NLP tools: Calling out to other libraries or APIs for specialized tasks.

Modifying existing annotations: Correcting or enhancing the output of default components.

Filtering or augmenting documents: Adding metadata or removing irrelevant information.

Here's an example of a custom component that identifies hashtags:

Python

```
import spacy

nlp = spacy.load("en_core_web_sm")

def hashtag_detector(doc):
    hashtags = []
    for token in doc:
        if token.text.startswith("#"):
            span = doc.char_span(token.idx, token.idx + len(token.text), label="HASHTAG")
            if span is not None:
                hashtags.append(span)
    doc.ents = list(doc.ents) + hashtags # Add hashtags to existing entities
    return doc

nlp.add_pipe(hashtag_detector,         name="hashtag_detector", after="tokenizer") # Add after the tokenizer

doc = nlp("Check out the latest #NLP trends and #spaCy tips!")
print(doc.ents)
for ent in doc.ents:
    print(ent.text, ent.label_)
```

In this example, the `hashtag_detector` component iterates through the tokens, identifies those starting with "#", creates entity spans with the label "HASHTAG", and adds them to the `doc.ents`.

By leveraging spaCy's component-based architecture, you gain fine-grained control over your NLP processing, enabling you to build highly specialized and efficient pipelines tailored to your specific application. This modularity also promotes code reusability and maintainability.

1.3   Optimizing Performance and Memory Management

Optimizing performance and memory management in spaCy is crucial for handling large datasets and deploying efficient NLP applications. Several strategies can be employed to achieve this:

1. Efficient Data Handling with `nlp.pipe`: As discussed earlier, using `nlp.pipe` for processing collections of texts is significantly more efficient than processing documents individually. It allows spaCy to work with internal data structures in batches, reducing Python overhead and improving speed. Remember to experiment with `batch_size` and `n_process` to find the optimal settings for your hardware.

2. Selective Component Loading and Disabling: Load only the language model and pipeline components you actually need. Disabling unnecessary components with the `disable` argument during model loading can drastically reduce memory footprint and processing time:

Python

import spacy

```
# Load only the tokenizer and NER
nlp_minimal = spacy.load("en_core_web_sm", disable=["tok2vec",
"tagger", "parser", "attribute_ruler", "lemmatizer"])
print(nlp_minimal.pipeline)

# Load with a custom pipeline configuration
config = {
    "nlp": {
        "pipeline": [
            {"name": "tokenizer"},
            {"name": "ner"}
        ]
    }
}
nlp_custom = spacy.load("en_core_web_sm", config=config)
print(nlp_custom.pipeline)
```

3. Processing Large Texts in Chunks: For very long documents, processing them in smaller chunks can prevent memory issues. You can iterate through sentences or paragraphs and process them individually or in smaller batches.

Python

```
import spacy

nlp = spacy.load("en_core_web_sm")
long_text = "This is a very long text. " * 1000

doc = nlp(long_text) # This might consume a lot of memory

# Process in sentences
for sent in doc.sents:
    # Process each sentence
    print(sent.text[:50])
```

4. Utilizing Generators for Large Datasets: When dealing with massive text corpora that don't fit into memory, use generators to stream data to `nlp.pipe`. This avoids loading the entire dataset into RAM at once (as demonstrated in the "Designing for High-Throughput Text Processing" explanation).

5. Managing Vocabulary and String Store: spaCy's `StringStore` efficiently stores all unique strings (words, labels, etc.) only once. However, if you're building many `Doc` objects with overlapping vocabulary, ensure you're reusing the same `nlp` object to benefit from this shared storage. Creating a new `nlp` object for each processing task can lead to memory duplication.

6. Freeing Up Memory: In long-running processes, you might want to explicitly delete `Doc` objects after you're done with them to release the associated memory:

Python

```
import spacy
import gc

nlp = spacy.load("en_core_web_sm")
texts = ["Some text " * 100] * 1000

for doc in nlp.pipe(texts):
    # Process the doc
    print(doc.ents)
    del doc # Explicitly delete the Doc object
gc.collect() # Force garbage collection
```

While Python's garbage collector usually handles memory management, explicitly deleting large objects and triggering garbage collection can be helpful in memory-constrained environments.

7. Choosing the Right Language Model: Larger language models (e.g., `en_core_web_lg`) generally offer higher accuracy but consume more memory and are slower than smaller models (e.g., `en_core_web_sm`). Choose the smallest model that meets your accuracy requirements.

8. Utilizing Hardware Acceleration (GPU): For computationally intensive tasks, especially those involving transformer models, leveraging a GPU with libraries like `cupy` can significantly improve processing speed. spaCy has experimental support for GPU usage.

9. Profiling Your Code: Use profiling tools (like `cProfile` in Python) to identify bottlenecks in your code. This can help you pinpoint which parts of your pipeline are consuming the most time and memory, allowing you to focus your optimization efforts effectively.

By implementing these strategies, you can build spaCy pipelines that are both performant and memory-efficient, enabling you to process large volumes of text data effectively. Remember that the optimal approach often depends on the specific task, dataset size, and available hardware resources.

CHAPTER 2

Mastering Custom Components and Extensions

2.1 Building Reusable and Shareable spaCy Components

Building reusable and shareable spaCy components is essential for creating modular, maintainable, and collaborative NLP workflows. SpaCy's design encourages the creation of custom components that can be easily integrated into different pipelines and shared across projects or with the wider community. Here's how you can build and package such components:

1. Defining Your Component as a Callable:

A spaCy pipeline component is essentially a Python callable (a function or a class with a `__call__` method) that takes a Doc object as input, modifies it, and returns the modified Doc.

```python
Python

from spacy.language import Language
from spacy.tokens import Doc

@Language.factory(
    "custom_length_detector",
    default_config={"min_length": 10}
)
def create_length_detector(nlp: Language, name: str, min_length:
int):
    def length_detector(doc: Doc) -> Doc:
```

```
        long_tokens = [token for token in doc if len(token.text) >=
min_length]
        if long_tokens:
            print(f"Document contains long tokens: {[token.text for
token in long_tokens]}")
        return doc
    return length_detector


# Load a base model
nlp = spacy.load("en_core_web_sm")

# Add the custom component to the pipeline
nlp.add_pipe("custom_length_detector", config={"min_length": 15})

doc = nlp("This is a short sentence. This one is significantly longer
and has more words.")
```

In this example:

We use the `@Language.factory` decorator to register our component with spaCy. This makes it easy to add to a pipeline by its string name ("custom_length_detector").

`default_config` allows users to customize the component's behavior when adding it to the pipeline.

`create_length_detector` is the factory function that takes the `nlp` object, the component name, and any configuration as arguments and returns the actual component function (`length_detector`).

The `length_detector` function takes a `Doc` object, performs its logic, and returns the modified `Doc`.

2. Packaging Your Component:

To make your component reusable and shareable, you should package it as a Python package. This involves creating a standard Python project structure:

```
my_custom_components/
├── __init__.py
└── my_component.py
```

In `my_component.py`, you would define your component factory:

Python

```python
from spacy.language import Language
from spacy.tokens import Doc

@Language.factory(
    "fancy_entity_highlighter",
    default_config={"color": "yellow"}
)
def create_fancy_highlighter(nlp: Language, name: str, color: str):
    def fancy_highlighter(doc: Doc) -> Doc:
        for ent in doc.ents:
            print(f"Entity '{ent.text}' ({ent.label_}) will be highlighted in {color}.")
        return doc
    return fancy_highlighter
```

In `__init__.py`, you would typically import and potentially register your factories:

Python

```python
from .my_component import create_fancy_highlighter
```

3. Installing and Using Your Packaged Component:

Users can install your package using pip:

Bash

```
pip install path/to/my_custom_components
```

Once installed, they can load a spaCy model and add your custom component by its registered name:

Python

```
import spacy

nlp = spacy.load("en_core_web_sm")
nlp.add_pipe("fancy_entity_highlighter",        config={"color": "lightblue"})

doc = nlp("Apple is looking at buying U.K. startup for $1 billion.")
```

4. Sharing Your Component:

You can share your components in several ways:

Within your organization: By distributing the Python package internally.

Open source: By publishing your package on platforms like PyPI (Python Package Index) so that anyone can install and use it. This makes your work accessible to the wider NLP community.

Through spaCy Universe: The spaCy Universe (https://spacy.io/universe) is a curated list of third-party packages and projects for spaCy. You can contribute your well-documented and tested components to the Universe to increase their visibility.

Best Practices for Reusability and Sharing:

Clear Naming: Use descriptive and unique names for your component and its factory.

Configuration Options: Provide sensible default configurations and allow users to customize behavior through the `config` argument.

Documentation: Thoroughly document your component's purpose, usage, configuration options, and any dependencies.

Testing: Write unit tests to ensure your component functions correctly under various conditions.

Type Hinting: Use type hints for better code readability and maintainability.

Error Handling: Implement robust error handling to make your component more reliable.

By following these guidelines, you can create spaCy components that are not only effective for your specific tasks but also valuable and easy to use for others in the NLP community. This fosters collaboration and accelerates the development of specialized NLP capabilities.

2.2 Extending spaCy's Functionality with Custom Attributes

Extending spaCy's functionality with custom attributes allows you to add your own information and properties to spaCy's core data

structures: Doc, Token, Span, and Lexeme. This is incredibly useful for annotating text with domain-specific information, precomputed features, or the results of custom analysis.
SpaCy provides two main ways to define custom attributes:

1. Extension Properties (Recommended for most use cases):

Extension properties are registered on the respective classes (Doc, Token, Span, Lexeme) and can be accessed like built-in attributes (e.g., doc._.my_attribute). They can be simple values, getter functions (computed dynamically), or setter functions (allowing you to modify the underlying object based on the attribute value).

a) Token Extensions:

Python

```
import spacy
from spacy.tokens import Token

# Define a custom attribute to check if a token is a stopword in a custom list
custom_stopwords = {"thee", "thou"}

def is_custom_stopword(token):
    return token.text.lower() in custom_stopwords

Token.set_extension("is_my_stop",    getter=is_custom_stopword,
force=True)

nlp = spacy.load("en_core_web_sm")
doc = nlp("To be or not to be, that is the question, whether 'tis nobler in the mind to suffer.")

for token in doc:
```

```
                    print(f"{token.text}:      is_stop={token.is_stop},
is_my_stop={token._.is_my_stop}")
```

Here, we define a token extension `is_my_stop` that uses a getter function to check against our `custom_stopwords` set. `force=True` allows overwriting an existing extension if there's a name collision (use with caution).

b) Span Extensions:

Python

```python
import spacy
from spacy.tokens import Span

def get_span_length(span):
    return len(span)

Span.set_extension("length", getter=get_span_length, force=True)

nlp = spacy.load("en_core_web_sm")
doc = nlp("London is the capital and largest city of England and the United Kingdom.")

for ent in doc.ents:
    print(f"{ent.text}: length={ent._.length}")
```

This example adds a `length` attribute to spans, calculated by a getter function.

c) Doc Extensions:

Python

```python
import spacy
from spacy.tokens import Doc

def count_sentences(doc):
    return len(list(doc.sents))

Doc.set_extension("sentence_count",        getter=count_sentences,
force=True)

nlp = spacy.load("en_core_web_sm")
doc = nlp("This is the first sentence. Here is the second one!")
print(f"Sentence count: {doc._.sentence_count}")
```

Here, we add a `sentence_count` attribute to the `Doc` object using a getter.

d) Setting Values Directly:

You can also set extension values directly, without a getter or setter:

Python

```python
import spacy
from spacy.tokens import Doc

Doc.set_extension("source", default=None, force=True)

nlp = spacy.load("en_core_web_sm")
doc1 = nlp("Some text.")
doc1._.source = "Web article"
print(f"Doc 1 source: {doc1._.source}")

doc2 = nlp("Another piece of text.")
print(f"Doc 2 source: {doc2._.source}") # Will be None (the default)
```

e) Setter Functions:

Setter functions allow you to define custom logic when an extension attribute is assigned a value:

Python

```python
import spacy
from spacy.tokens import Token

def set_token_sentiment(token, sentiment):
    token._.sentiment_score = sentiment

Token.set_extension("sentiment_score", default=0.0, force=True)
Token.set_extension("sentiment", setter=set_token_sentiment, force=True)

nlp = spacy.load("en_core_web_sm")
doc = nlp("This is a great day!")
doc[3]._.sentiment = 0.9 # Setting the 'sentiment' attribute triggers the setter
print(f"{doc[3].text}: Sentiment Score = {doc[3]._.sentiment_score}")
```

2. User Data (doc.user_data, token.user_data, span.user_data):

Each Doc, Token, and Span object also has a .user_data attribute, which is a simple dictionary where you can store arbitrary Python objects. This is less structured than extension properties but can be useful for attaching temporary or complex data.

Python

```python
import spacy

nlp = spacy.load("en_core_web_sm")
doc = nlp("This is a test.")
doc.user_data["file_name"] = "test.txt"
doc[2].user_data["is_important"] = True

print(f"Doc source: {doc.user_data['file_name']}")
print(f"Token 'is' important: {doc[2].user_data.get('is_important', False)}")
```

Choosing Between Extension Properties and User Data:

Extension Properties: Preferred for adding well-defined attributes with potential getter, setter, or default behavior. They are more integrated into spaCy's object model.

User Data: Useful for attaching arbitrary, transient data without defining a specific structure. Less formal but can be convenient for quick annotations.

By leveraging custom attributes, you can enrich spaCy's linguistic annotations with your own domain-specific information, making your NLP pipelines more powerful and tailored to your unique needs. This is a fundamental technique for advanced spaCy usage.

2.3 Integrating External Libraries Seamlessly

Integrating external libraries seamlessly with spaCy allows you to leverage the strengths of other specialized tools within your NLP pipelines. SpaCy's flexible architecture makes it possible to incorporate libraries for tasks like sentiment analysis, topic modeling, knowledge graph construction, or even integration with machine learning frameworks. Here are several strategies and examples for achieving this:

1. Within Custom Pipeline Components:

The most common and recommended way to integrate external libraries is within custom spaCy pipeline components. You can define a component that takes a Doc object, uses the external library to perform some analysis, and then adds the results back to the Doc (either as custom attributes or within `doc.user_data`).

Example: Integrating a Sentiment Analysis Library (e.g., VADER):

Python

```
import spacy
from spacy.language import Language
from spacy.tokens import Doc
from vaderSentiment.vaderSentiment import SentimentIntensityAnalyzer

@Language.factory("vader_sentiment")
def create_vader_sentiment(nlp: Language, name: str):
    analyzer = SentimentIntensityAnalyzer()
    def vader_sentiment(doc: Doc) -> Doc:
        scores = analyzer.polarity_scores(doc.text)
        doc._.sentiment = scores
        return doc
    Doc.set_extension("sentiment", default=None, force=True)
    return vader_sentiment

nlp = spacy.load("en_core_web_sm")
nlp.add_pipe("vader_sentiment")

doc = nlp("This is a fantastic and amazing product! I am so happy.")
```

```
print(doc.__.sentiment)
```

In this example, we create a custom pipeline component `vader_sentiment` that uses the `vaderSentiment` library to get polarity scores for the entire document and stores them as a custom Doc attribute.

2. Processing within `nlp.pipe`:

If the external library can process text efficiently, you can integrate it within the processing loop of `nlp.pipe`. This is useful when you need to apply an external function to each document in a large corpus.

Example: Using a hypothetical function from an external library:

Python

```python
import spacy
from your_external_lib import analyze_text # Hypothetical library

nlp = spacy.load("en_core_web_sm")

def process_with_external(doc):
    external_results = analyze_text(doc.text)
    doc.user_data["external_analysis"] = external_results
    return doc

texts = ["Some text to analyze.", "Another piece of text."]
for doc in nlp.pipe(texts, function=process_with_external):
    print(doc.user_data.get("external_analysis"))
```

Here, we pass a custom function `process_with_external` to the `function` argument of `nlp.pipe`. This function receives each `Doc` object and can interact with the external library.

3. Leveraging Callbacks in Custom Components:

For more complex interactions, you might use callbacks within your custom components. For instance, you could have a component that identifies certain entities and then uses an external knowledge graph library to enrich those entities.

Example (Conceptual):

Python

```python
import spacy
from spacy.language import Language
from spacy.tokens import Doc
from your_kg_lib import query_knowledge_graph # Hypothetical library

@Language.factory("kg_enricher")
def create_kg_enricher(nlp: Language, name: str, kg_endpoint: str):
    def kg_enricher(doc: Doc) -> Doc:
        for ent in doc.ents:
            if ent.label_ in ["ORG", "PERSON", "LOC"]:
                entity_data = query_knowledge_graph(ent.text, endpoint=kg_endpoint)
                ent._.kg_data = entity_data
        return doc
    Doc.set_extension("kg_data", default=None, force=True)
    return kg_enricher

nlp = spacy.load("en_core_web_sm")
nlp.add_pipe("ner") # Ensure NER is run before our component
```

```
nlp.add_pipe("kg_enricher",                    config={"kg_endpoint":
"http://example.com/kg"})

doc = nlp("Apple is headquartered in Cupertino.")
for ent in doc.ents:
    print(f"{ent.text}: {ent._.kg_data}")
```

4. Using External Libraries for Pre- or Post-processing:

Sometimes, it's more efficient to use an external library to process text *before* it enters the spaCy pipeline or to analyze the output *after* spaCy has done its work.

Example: Pre-processing with a text normalization library:

Python

```
import spacy
from text_normalization_lib import normalize_text # Hypothetical
library

nlp = spacy.load("en_core_web_sm")
raw_text = "This is  some text with  extra  spaces."
normalized_text = normalize_text(raw_text)
doc = nlp(normalized_text)
print(doc.text)
```

Best Practices for Seamless Integration:

Encapsulation: Keep the interaction with the external library within your custom component or processing function. This makes your spaCy pipeline more self-contained and easier to understand.

Data Conversion: Be mindful of how data is passed between spaCy's Doc, Token, and Span objects and the data structures expected by the external library. You might need to perform some data conversion.

Error Handling: Implement robust error handling to gracefully manage potential issues with the external library (e.g., API errors, unexpected output).

Configuration: If your integration requires specific settings for the external library, consider making these configurable parameters of your custom component.

Documentation: Clearly document how your component interacts with the external library and any dependencies.

By following these strategies, you can effectively integrate the specialized capabilities of external libraries into your spaCy pipelines, creating powerful and versatile NLP solutions. The key is to design your integration in a modular and maintainable way, leveraging spaCy's component-based architecture.

CHAPTER 3

Advanced Tokenization and Subword Techniques

3.1 Implementing Custom Tokenization Strategies

Implementing custom tokenization strategies in spaCy allows you to handle text in ways that go beyond the default tokenization rules. This is particularly useful for languages with different writing systems, domain-specific text with unusual formatting, or when you need fine-grained control over how text is split into meaningful units.

SpaCy's tokenization process is highly configurable. You can customize it at different levels:

1. Rule-Based Tokenization with Language Data:

For many languages, spaCy relies on language-specific data that defines rules for tokenization (e.g., prefixes, suffixes, infixes, word boundaries). You can modify this data to adjust the default behavior.

`tokenizer_exceptions`: These are special-case rules for tokens that should be split or kept together in a non-standard way (e.g., "don't" should be split into "do" and "n't").

`prefix_search`, `suffix_search`, `infix_finditer`: These regular expressions define patterns for prefixes, suffixes, and infixes that should be split off.

`token_match`: An optional function to match tokens based on custom criteria.

You can customize these rules when creating or loading a language model:

Python

```python
import spacy
from spacy.lang.en import English

# Get the default English language data
nlp = English()
tokenizer = nlp.tokenizer

# Add a tokenizer exception for a specific case
special_cases = [{"ORTH": "example.com"}]
tokenizer.add_special_case(special_cases)

# Modify prefix rules (add a custom prefix)
prefix_re = spacy.util.compile_prefix_regex(English.Defaults.prefixes + ("@",))
tokenizer.prefix_search = prefix_re.search

doc = nlp("@user Hello example.com")
for token in doc:
    print(token.text)
```

While powerful, directly modifying language data requires a good understanding of spaCy's internal tokenization process and can be complex for intricate rules.

2. Creating a Custom Tokenizer Function:

For more complex or entirely different tokenization logic, you can define a custom tokenizer function and replace the default tokenizer in your `nlp` object. Your custom function should take a text string as input and return a `Doc` object. You'll need to handle the tokenization process yourself and then create the `Doc` object using `nlp.make_doc()`.

Python

```python
import spacy
from spacy.language import Language
from spacy.tokens import Doc

@Language.factory("custom_tokenizer")
def create_custom_tokenizer(nlp: Language, name: str):
    def custom_tokenizer(text: str) -> Doc:
        # Your custom tokenization logic here
        tokens = text.split("***") # Example: Split by "***"
        spaces = [False] * len(tokens) # Indicate if there's a space after each token
        return Doc(nlp.vocab, words=tokens, spaces=spaces)
    return custom_tokenizer

# Load a base model (or create an empty one)
nlp = spacy.blank("en")

# Add the custom tokenizer to the pipeline as the first component
nlp.add_pipe("custom_tokenizer",        name="custom_tokenizer",
first=True)

doc = nlp("This***is***some***text")
for token in doc:
    print(token.text)
```

In this example:

We define a factory function `create_custom_tokenizer` that returns our `custom_tokenizer` function.

The `custom_tokenizer` function splits the input text by "***".

We create a `Doc` object using `nlp.vocab`, the extracted tokens, and a list indicating whitespace after each token (important for correct span indexing).

We add this custom tokenizer as the very first component in the pipeline using `first=True`.

3. Using a Subclass of the `Tokenizer`:

You can also create a custom tokenizer by subclassing spaCy's `Tokenizer` class. This gives you more direct access to the internal methods and attributes of the tokenizer.

Python

```python
import spacy
from spacy.tokenizer import Tokenizer
from spacy.lang.en import English

class MyTokenizer(Tokenizer):
        def __init__(self, vocab, special_cases=None, prefix_search=None,
                    suffix_search=None, infix_finditer=None,
token_match=None):
            super().__init__(vocab, special_cases, prefix_search,
suffix_search,
                    infix_finditer, token_match)
```

```python
def __call__(self, text):
    # Custom tokenization logic
    words = text.replace("-", " ").split() # Example: Split by spaces
after replacing hyphens
    spaces = [True] * len(words)
    return self.make_doc(words, spaces)

# Load a base model and replace its tokenizer
nlp = English()
nlp.tokenizer = MyTokenizer(nlp.vocab)

doc = nlp("multi-word expression")
for token in doc:
    print(token.text)
```

Here, we create a `MyTokenizer` class that overrides the `__call__` method to implement our custom tokenization. We then replace the default tokenizer of our `nlp` object with an instance of `MyTokenizer`.

Considerations When Implementing Custom Tokenization:

Whitespace Handling: Ensure your custom tokenizer correctly identifies and handles whitespace, as this is crucial for accurate span creation and indexing in the `Doc` object. The `spaces` list passed to `Doc` indicates whether a token is followed by whitespace.

Special Cases: Consider how you want to handle special cases like contractions, URLs, email addresses, etc. You might need to implement specific rules for these.

Integration with Downstream Components: Be aware that custom tokenization can affect the performance and accuracy of subsequent pipeline components (e.g., tagger, parser, NER), as they are trained on spaCy's default tokenization scheme. You might need to retrain these components on data tokenized with your custom strategy.

Performance: Complex custom tokenization logic can impact processing speed. Optimize your code for efficiency, especially when dealing with large volumes of text.

Implementing custom tokenization provides a high degree of flexibility in how spaCy processes text, allowing you to tailor it precisely to your specific linguistic needs and data formats. Choose the method that best suits the complexity of your requirements.

3.2 Exploring Subword Tokenization for Complex Languages

Subword tokenization is a crucial technique in Natural Language Processing (NLP), especially when dealing with complex languages characterized by rich morphology (e.g., agglutinative languages like Turkish, Finnish, Hungarian) or a large number of possible word forms.[1] Traditional word-based tokenization often struggles with such languages due to:

Large Vocabulary Size: The number of unique word forms can be enormous, leading to very large vocabularies that are difficult for models to handle efficiently.

Out-of-Vocabulary (OOV) Words: New or rare word forms not seen during training are common, leading to the OOV problem where the model cannot process them.[2]

Data Sparsity: Many word forms might appear very infrequently in the training data, making it hard for the model to learn reliable representations for them.[3]

Subword tokenization addresses these challenges by breaking down words into smaller, more frequent units called subwords. These subwords can be morphemes (meaningful units like prefixes, suffixes, roots) or simply frequent character sequences.[4] This approach offers several advantages for complex languages:

Advantages of Subword Tokenization for Complex Languages:

Reduced Vocabulary Size: By representing words as combinations of subwords, the total vocabulary size needed to cover a large portion of the language can be significantly smaller than a word-based vocabulary.

Handling OOV Words: When a new word is encountered, it can often be broken down into known subword units, allowing the model to understand and process it to some extent, even if the whole word was not seen during training.

Improved Representation of Morphological Variations: Subword units can capture the underlying morphemes of a language.[5] For example, in Turkish, the word "geliyorlar" (they are coming) might be broken into "gel-iyor-lar", where each part carries a specific meaning.[6] This helps the model understand the relationships between different word forms.

Mitigating Data Sparsity: Subword units are generally more frequent than full word forms, especially for morphologically rich languages. This increased frequency allows the model to learn better and more robust representations for these units.

Better Generalization: By understanding the meaning conveyed by subword units, models can generalize better to new words and word forms they haven't seen before.[7]

Common Subword Tokenization Algorithms:

Several algorithms are used for subword tokenization, including:

Byte-Pair Encoding (BPE): This algorithm starts with individual characters as the initial vocabulary and iteratively merges the most frequent adjacent character or subword pairs until a desired vocabulary size is reached.[8]

WordPiece: Similar to BPE, WordPiece also iteratively merges subword units.[9] However, instead of merging based on frequency, it merges the pair that maximizes the likelihood of the training data.[10]

Unigram Language Model: This approach starts with a large vocabulary of all possible subwords and iteratively removes the subword that causes the smallest decrease in the likelihood of the training data.[11]

SentencePiece: This library implements both BPE and Unigram algorithms and treats the input text as a raw sequence, without relying on pre-tokenization based on spaces.[12] It can handle languages without clear word boundaries more effectively.[13]

spaCy and Subword Tokenization:

As of the current version, spaCy's core tokenization is primarily rule-based and language-specific, focusing on splitting text into words and punctuation based on predefined rules and exceptions.[14] **spaCy does not natively implement subword tokenization algorithms like BPE or WordPiece directly within its core pipeline.**

However, you can integrate subword tokenization into your spaCy workflows by:

1.Pre-processing the text: Use an external library like Hugging Face's `tokenizers` or SentencePiece to tokenize your text into subword units *before* feeding it into a spaCy pipeline.[15] You would then need to adapt how you create `Doc` objects from these subword tokens, potentially using custom components.

2. Custom Tokenizer: You could potentially create a highly custom tokenizer in spaCy that mimics some aspects of subword tokenization, but this would require significant effort and might not fully replicate the benefits of established algorithms like BPE.

3. Using Transformer Models: When using transformer models via libraries like `spacy-transformers`, the tokenization is handled by the specific transformer model's tokenizer (e.g., WordPiece for BERT).[16] In this case, spaCy acts as a wrapper around these models, and the subword tokenization is an inherent part of the transformer's processing.

Example (Conceptual with Hugging Face `tokenizers`):

Python

```
from tokenizers import BytePairEncoding

# Train a BPE tokenizer on your corpus
tokenizer = BytePairEncoding(
    vocab_size=10000,
    min_frequency=2,
    special_tokens=["[UNK]", "[CLS]", "[SEP]", "[PAD]", "[MASK]"]
)
# Assuming 'corpus.txt' is your training data
tokenizer.train(['corpus.txt'])
```

```
# Load a spaCy model
import spacy
nlp = spacy.blank("xx") # Multi-language model

def custom_tokenizer(text):
    encoded = tokenizer.encode(text).tokens
    # Need to create a spaCy Doc object from these tokens
    # This would require careful handling of whitespace and token
attributes
    words = encoded
    spaces = [True] * len(words) # Naive whitespace assumption
            doc  =  spacy.tokens.Doc(nlp.vocab,  words=words,
spaces=spaces)
    return doc

nlp.tokenizer = custom_tokenizer

doc = nlp("Bu çok karmaşık bir dil.") # This is a very complex
language (Turkish)
for token in doc:
    print(token.text)
```

In summary, while spaCy's core doesn't directly implement subword tokenization, you can effectively leverage it for complex languages by integrating external subword tokenization libraries into your pre-processing steps or by using transformer models within spaCy, where subword tokenization is a standard part of their architecture. Understanding subword tokenization is crucial for achieving state-of-the-art results in NLP tasks for morphologically rich and other complex languages.[17]

3.3 Handling Non-Standard Text Formats Effectively

Handling non-standard text formats effectively with spaCy requires a flexible approach that often involves a combination of custom preprocessing, tailored tokenization, and careful design of your NLP pipeline. Non-standard formats can include a wide range of variations, such as:

Text with unusual delimiters: Instead of spaces, other characters might separate words or meaningful units.

Structured text within free text: Log files, code snippets, or specific markup might be embedded in natural language.

Inconsistent formatting: Variations in spacing, capitalization, or the use of special characters.

Domain-specific notations: Scientific formulas, medical codes, or financial tickers.

OCR errors or noisy text: Text extracted from images might contain errors or inconsistencies.

Here's a breakdown of strategies to tackle these challenges effectively:

1. Preprocessing and Normalization:

Before feeding non-standard text into a spaCy pipeline, it's often crucial to preprocess and normalize it to create a more consistent and analyzable format. This might involve:

Regular Expression Manipulation: Use re module in Python to identify and replace or extract specific patterns. For example, you might need to:

Replace multiple whitespace characters with single spaces.

Remove or normalize special characters.

Extract structured data embedded within the text.

Handle domain-specific notations.

Python

```python
import re
text = "This   text  has\tmultiple\nspaces."
normalized_text = re.sub(r'\s+', ' ', text).strip()
print(f"Original: '{text}'")
print(f"Normalized: '{normalized_text}'")

log_entry = "[ERROR] 2023-10-27 10:00:00 - Failed to connect"
timestamp = re.search(r'\[(.*?)\]', log_entry).group(1)
message = re.search(r' - (.*)', log_entry).group(1)
print(f"Timestamp: {timestamp}, Message: {message}")
```

Decoding and Encoding: Ensure the text is in the correct encoding (e.g., UTF-8). Handle potential decoding errors.

Case Normalization: Convert text to lowercase or uppercase to reduce variations.

Handling Domain-Specific Formats: Write specific functions or rules to parse and transform domain-specific notations into a more standard format that spaCy can process.

2. Custom Tokenization:

The default spaCy tokenizer might not work well with non-standard formats. Implementing custom tokenization strategies becomes essential:

Tokenizer Exceptions: Add special cases to handle specific tokens that should be treated differently (e.g., multi-word expressions separated by hyphens that you want to keep as single tokens).

Custom Tokenizer Function: As discussed previously, you can create a completely custom tokenizer function that splits the text based on your specific rules and delimiters. This is particularly useful when the text doesn't follow standard whitespace-based tokenization.

Python

```python
import spacy
from spacy.language import Language
from spacy.tokens import Doc

@Language.factory("code_tokenizer")
def create_code_tokenizer(nlp: Language, name: str):
    def code_tokenizer(text: str) -> Doc:
        tokens = re.findall(r"[\w.]+|[^\w\s.]", text) # Split by word
characters, dots, or other non-whitespace
        spaces = [False] * len(tokens)
        return Doc(nlp.vocab, words=tokens, spaces=spaces)
```

```
    return code_tokenizer

nlp = spacy.blank("en")
nlp.add_pipe("code_tokenizer",                name="code_tokenizer",
first=True)
code_text = "variable.name = function(arg1, arg2);"
doc = nlp(code_text)
for token in doc:
    print(token.text)
```

Subword Tokenization (Indirectly): If your non-standard text contains many unknown or domain-specific terms, consider pre-tokenizing it into subwords using external libraries before feeding it into spaCy.

3. Adapting the NLP Pipeline:

The default spaCy pipeline components (tagger, parser, NER) are trained on standard text. They might not perform well on non-standard formats. You might need to:

Train Custom Models: If you have annotated data in your non-standard format, you can train custom spaCy models (tagger, parser, NER) specifically for this data. This will allow the model to learn the patterns and structures inherent in the format.

Rule-Based Components: For certain tasks like entity recognition in structured text within free text, rule-based components (`Matcher`, `PhraseMatcher`) might be more effective and robust than statistical models. You can write patterns that specifically target the structures and keywords in your non-standard format.

Python

```
import spacy
from spacy.matcher import Matcher

nlp = spacy.load("en_core_web_sm")
matcher = Matcher(nlp.vocab)
pattern = [{"TEXT": "["}, {"TEXT": "ERROR"}, {"TEXT": "]"},
{"TEXT": {"IS_DIGIT": True}}, {"TEXT": "-"}, {"TEXT": {"IS_DIGIT":
True}}]
matcher.add("LOG_ERROR", [pattern])

log_line = "[ERROR] 12345-67890 - Something went wrong"
doc = nlp(log_line)
matches = matcher(doc)
for match_id, start, end in matches:
    span = doc[start:end]
    print(f"Found error code: {span.text}")
```

Conditional Pipeline Components: You might want to have different pipeline branches or conditional execution of components based on the format of the input text. This can be achieved by writing custom components that inspect the Doc object and decide whether to apply certain processing steps.

4. Handling OCR Errors and Noisy Text:

If you're dealing with text extracted from images (OCR), you might encounter various errors. Strategies to handle this include:

Error Correction: Use spell-checking or error correction libraries to try and fix common OCR mistakes.

Fuzzy Matching: When trying to identify known entities or patterns, use fuzzy matching techniques to account for slight variations due to errors.

Training on Noisy Data: If you have enough noisy data, you can fine-tune spaCy models on this data to make them more robust to OCR errors.

Key Considerations:

Understand the Format: The first step is always to thoroughly understand the structure and characteristics of your non-standard text format.

Iterative Approach: Handling non-standard formats often requires an iterative approach. You might need to experiment with different preprocessing techniques, tokenization strategies, and pipeline configurations to find what works best for your specific data.

Domain Knowledge: Domain-specific knowledge is often crucial for effectively parsing and interpreting non-standard text.

Evaluation: Carefully evaluate the performance of your NLP pipeline on the non-standard data to ensure that your handling strategies are effective.

By combining these techniques, you can build robust and effective NLP pipelines for a wide range of non-standard text formats, unlocking valuable insights from data that might otherwise be difficult to analyze.

CHAPTER 4

Deep Dive into Entity Recognition and Linking

4.1 Fine-Tuning spaCy's NER Models for Specific Domains

Fine-tuning spaCy's Named Entity Recognition (NER) models for specific domains is a crucial step to achieve high accuracy when dealing with terminology and entities that are unique or have different contexts compared to the data the base spaCy models were trained on (typically news and web text). Here's a comprehensive guide on how to effectively fine-tune spaCy's NER models:

1. Data Preparation and Annotation:

Gather Domain-Specific Data: The most critical step is to collect a corpus of text relevant to your target domain. This could include research papers, medical records, legal documents, financial reports, social media posts related to a specific topic, etc. The more data you have, the better the potential for fine-tuning.

Annotation: You need to annotate your data with the entities you want your model to recognize. SpaCy's training format requires a list of tuples for each document, where each tuple contains the start and end character indices of an entity and its label. Tools like Doccano, Prodigy (from the creators of spaCy), or even custom scripts can be used for annotation.

Python

```
TRAIN_DATA = [
    ("Patient John Doe presented with symptoms of fever and
cough.", {"entities": [(0, 14, "PERSON"), (33, 38, "SYMPTOM"),
(44, 49, "SYMPTOM")]}),
    ("The company Acme Corp reported a revenue of $1 million.",
{"entities": [(12, 22, "ORG"), (41, 50, "MONEY")]}),
    ("Dr. Jane Smith prescribed 500mg of Paracetamol.", {"entities":
[(0, 13, "PERSON"), (30, 41, "DRUG")]}),
]
```

Data Splitting: Divide your annotated data into training, validation, and optionally, a test set. The validation set is crucial for monitoring performance during training and preventing overfitting.

2. Setting Up the Training Configuration:

SpaCy uses a configuration file (`.cfg`) to define all aspects of the training process, including the base model, pipeline components, optimization parameters, and evaluation metrics. You can create a custom configuration file or modify an existing one (e.g., by using `spacy init config` command in the terminal). Key parameters to consider:

`base_model`: Specify the pre-trained spaCy model you want to fine-tune (e.g., `en_core_web_sm`, `en_core_web_md`). Choose a model that has a vocabulary and general linguistic understanding relevant to your domain.

`pipeline`: Ensure the `ner` component is included in the pipeline. You might want to disable other components if you're solely focused on NER to speed up training and reduce memory usage.

`[components.ner]`: This section contains the configuration for the NER component, including the model architecture (`model.type`), dropout rates, and loss function.

`[components.ner.model.entity_linker]`: If you also want to perform entity linking, configure this section.

`[training]`: This section defines parameters like the number of training iterations (`max_epochs`), batch size, learning rate, and the path to your training and validation data.

`[training.optimizer]`: Configure the optimization algorithm (e.g., Adam).

`[training.batcher]`: Define how the training data is batched.

`[training.logger]`: Set up logging during training.

`[nlp.vocab]`: You might need to specify a larger vocabulary size if your domain has many unique terms not present in the base model's vocabulary.

Example Configuration Snippet (simplified):

Ini, TOML

```
[training]
dev = "path/to/dev.spacy"
train = "path/to/train.spacy"
max_epochs = 30
batch_size = 32

[optimizer]
```

```
learn_rate = 0.001

[nlp]
lang = "en"
pipeline = ["ner"]

[components]

[components.ner]
factory = "ner"

[components.ner.model]
@architectures = "spacy.NER.v1"
dropout = 0.2
```

3. Converting Data to spaCy Format:

SpaCy's training process expects the data in `.spacy` format, which is a binary format for efficiency. You can convert your annotated JSON or other formats to `.spacy` using spaCy's `convert` command in the terminal or programmatically:

Python

```python
import spacy
from spacy.training import Example
from spacy.tokens import DocBin

def convert_to_spacy(train_data, output_path):
    nlp = spacy.blank("en") # Or load your base model if you need its vocab
    db = DocBin()
    for text, annotations in train_data:
        doc = nlp.make_doc(text)
        ents = []
```

```
      for start, end, label in annotations.get("entities", []):
         span = doc.char_span(start, end, label=label)
         if span is not None:
             ents.append(span)
         else:
             print(f"Skipping entity [{start}, {end}, {label}] in: {text}")
      doc.ents = ents
      db.add(doc)
   db.to_disk(output_path)


convert_to_spacy(TRAIN_DATA, "train.spacy")
# Repeat for your development/validation data
```

4. Running the Training:

Once your configuration file is set up and your data is in `.spacy` format, you can start the fine-tuning process using the `spacy train` command in the terminal:

Bash

```
python -m spacy train config.cfg --output ./output --gpu-id 0
```

`config.cfg`: Your training configuration file.

`--output ./output`: The directory where the trained model will be saved.

`--gpu-id 0`: (Optional) Use GPU 0 for training if available.

SpaCy will iterate through the training data, update the model's weights based on the annotations, and evaluate its performance on the development/validation set after each epoch. Monitor the loss and evaluation metrics to determine when the model is performing well and to avoid overfitting.

5. Evaluation and Iteration:

After training, evaluate your fine-tuned model on a held-out test set to get an unbiased estimate of its performance. SpaCy provides various metrics like precision, recall, and F1-score for each entity type.

Python

```python
import spacy
from spacy.scorer import Scorer
from spacy.training import Example

def evaluate_model(nlp, test_data):
    scorer = Scorer()
    examples = []
    for text, annotations in test_data:
        doc = nlp(text)
        example = Example.from_dict(doc, annotations)
        examples.append(example)
    scores = scorer.score(examples)
    return scores

# Load your trained model
trained_nlp = spacy.load("./output/model-best")
test_scores = evaluate_model(trained_nlp, TEST_DATA)
print(test_scores)
```

Based on the evaluation results, you might need to iterate on your data (e.g., annotate more data, correct errors), adjust your training configuration (e.g., learning rate, number of epochs), or even try a different base model.

6. Saving and Using the Fine-Tuned Model:

Once you are satisfied with the performance, you can save the best version of your trained model:

Python

```python
output_path = "./fine_tuned_model"
trained_nlp.to_disk(output_path)
print(f"Saved fine-tuned model to {output_path}")

# Load and use the fine-tuned model
loaded_nlp = spacy.load(output_path)
doc = loaded_nlp("Patient John Doe was treated with Paracetamol for his fever.")
for ent in doc.ents:
    print(ent.text, ent.label_)
```

Key Considerations for Effective Fine-Tuning:

Data Quality and Quantity: High-quality, domain-relevant annotated data is the most crucial factor. The amount of data needed depends on the complexity of your domain and the number of entity types.

Choice of Base Model: Start with a base model that has a vocabulary and general understanding relevant to your domain. Larger models might offer better potential accuracy but require more data and computational resources.

Learning Rate and Other Hyperparameters: Experiment with different learning rates, batch sizes, and dropout rates in your training configuration. Use the validation set to tune these hyperparameters.

Overfitting: Monitor the performance on the validation set to detect overfitting (where the model performs well on the training data but poorly on unseen data). Adjust the number of epochs, dropout rate, or add regularization techniques to mitigate overfitting.

Catastrophic Forgetting: Fine-tuning can sometimes lead to the model forgetting previously learned information. Techniques like gradual unfreezing or using smaller learning rates for earlier layers can help mitigate this.

Transfer Learning: Fine-tuning is a form of transfer learning. You are leveraging the knowledge learned by the base model and adapting it to your specific domain.

By following these steps and considerations, you can effectively fine-tune spaCy's NER models to achieve high accuracy on your domain-specific text data. Remember that fine-tuning is often an iterative process that requires experimentation and careful evaluation.

4.2 Implementing Advanced Entity Linking Strategies

Implementing advanced entity linking strategies with spaCy goes beyond simply identifying named entities; it involves connecting those entities to entries in a knowledge base (KB) to disambiguate them and provide more contextual information. This is crucial for tasks like question answering, information retrieval, and knowledge graph construction. Here's a breakdown of advanced techniques and how to approach them with spaCy:

1. Leveraging spaCy's `EntityLinker` **Component:**

SpaCy has a built-in `EntityLinker` component (available in the `spacy-experimental` package and as a custom component in some pipelines) that can be trained to link entities to a knowledge base. This component typically relies on:

Candidate Generation: Identifying potential KB entries that could correspond to the detected entity mention. This often involves string matching, fuzzy matching, or using an inverted index of entity mentions in the KB.

Disambiguation: Ranking the candidate KB entries based on contextual information within the document. This can involve comparing the surrounding words, the entity types, and the relationships between entities in the text with the information stored in the KB.

To use and train spaCy's `EntityLinker`, you would typically:

Prepare a Knowledge Base: This KB needs to be in a structured format that spaCy can understand. It usually includes entity IDs, their surface forms (mentions), descriptions, and potentially relationships to other entities.

Annotate Data for Linking: Your training data needs to include not only entity spans but also the corresponding KB IDs they should be linked to.

Configure and Train the `EntityLinker`**:** This involves specifying the KB, the candidate generation method, and the disambiguation model in your spaCy configuration file.

Evaluate the Linker: Assess the accuracy of the linking process on a held-out dataset.

While powerful, training a full-fledged entity linker from scratch requires a significant amount of annotated data and a well-structured knowledge base.

2. Integrating External Entity Linking Libraries:

Given the complexity of building an entity linker, you might want to integrate existing, specialized libraries into your spaCy pipeline. Some popular options include:

DBpedia Spotlight: A tool for automatically annotating DBpedia URIs in text. You can call its API from a custom spaCy component.

Wikidata Linker: A Python library specifically for linking entities to Wikidata. You can integrate it into your pipeline to leverage Wikidata's vast knowledge graph.

Other custom or domain-specific linkers: Depending on your domain, there might be specialized knowledge bases and linking tools available.

Example: Integrating Wikidata Linker:

Python

```python
import spacy
from spacy.language import Language
from spacy.tokens import Doc
from wikidata_linker import WikidataLinker

@Language.factory("wikidata_linker")
def create_wikidata_linker(nlp: Language, name: str):
    wl = WikidataLinker()
    def wikidata_linking(doc: Doc) -> Doc:
        doc = wl(doc)
        return doc
```

```
    return wikidata_linker

nlp = spacy.load("en_core_web_sm")
nlp.add_pipe("ner") # Ensure NER is in the pipeline
nlp.add_pipe("wikidata_linker")

text = "Apple was founded by Steve Jobs and Steve Wozniak."
doc = nlp(text)

for ent in doc.ents:
    print(ent.text, ent.label_, ent._.wikidata_id, ent._.wikidata_label)
```

This example demonstrates how to create a custom spaCy component that uses the `WikidataLinker` library to add Wikidata IDs and labels to the recognized entities.

3. Rule-Based Entity Linking with Knowledge Bases:

For specific domains or when dealing with well-defined entities and their mentions, you can implement rule-based linking strategies using spaCy's `Matcher` and a structured knowledge base. This approach involves:

Creating a Knowledge Base of Entity Mentions and IDs: Store a mapping of entity surface forms (and their variations) to their unique IDs in your KB.

Using the `PhraseMatcher`**:** Efficiently match entity mentions in the text against the surface forms in your KB.

Adding Custom Attributes: When a match is found, add the corresponding KB ID as a custom attribute to the matched span.

Handling Ambiguity: If a mention can refer to multiple entities, you might need additional rules or contextual information to disambiguate.

Example: Rule-Based Linking to a Simple KB:

Python

```python
import spacy
from spacy.matcher import PhraseMatcher
from spacy.tokens import Span

nlp = spacy.load("en_core_web_sm")
matcher = PhraseMatcher(nlp.vocab)
kb = {
    "Apple Inc.": "Q312",
    "Steve Jobs": "Q11384",
    "Steve Wozniak": "Q48318",
    "United Kingdom": "Q145"
}

for entity, qid in kb.items():
    matcher.add(qid, [nlp(entity)])

def link_entities(doc):
    matches = matcher(doc)
    linked_ents = []
    for match_id, start, end in matches:
        span = Span(doc, start, end, label="ENTITY") # Or the
original entity label if available
        span._.kb_id = match_id
        linked_ents.append(span)
    doc.ents = list(doc.ents) + linked_ents # Add linked entities to
doc.ents
    return doc
```

```
nlp.add_pipe(link_entities, name="entity_linker", after="ner") # Run
after NER

text = "Apple Inc. was founded by Steve Jobs and Steve Wozniak,
and is located in the United States."
doc = nlp(text)

for ent in doc.ents:
    print(ent.text, ent.label_, ent._.get("kb_id"))
```

4. Advanced Disambiguation Techniques:

When dealing with ambiguous entity mentions, advanced
disambiguation strategies can significantly improve linking
accuracy:

Contextual Similarity: Calculate the semantic similarity between
the context of the entity mention in the text and the descriptions or
surrounding entities of candidate KB entries. You can use word
embeddings or transformer models for this.

Coherence and Relatedness: Consider the relationships
between the entities in the text and the relationships between their
corresponding KB entries within the knowledge graph. A linking
that results in a more coherent subgraph in the KB is often
preferred.

Machine Learning Classifiers: Train a classifier that takes
features like the entity mention, its context, and properties of the
candidate KB entries as input and predicts the correct KB ID.

Knowledge Graph Embeddings: Use embeddings of the
knowledge graph to measure the relatedness between entities and
their context.

5. Handling Ambiguity and Confidence Scores:

Advanced entity linking systems often provide confidence scores for their predictions. You should consider how to handle ambiguous cases (low confidence) and potentially defer linking or provide multiple possible links.

6. Iterative Linking and Reasoning:

In some cases, the linking of one entity can provide context that helps in linking other entities in the same document. Iterative linking approaches can refine the links based on the overall coherence of the linked entities within the knowledge graph.

Key Considerations for Advanced Entity Linking:

Knowledge Base Quality: The accuracy and coverage of your knowledge base are crucial for the success of entity linking.

Data Annotation: High-quality annotated data for training (if using machine learning-based linkers) is essential.

Computational Cost: Advanced disambiguation techniques can be computationally expensive, especially when dealing with large knowledge bases and complex models.

Domain Specificity: The best entity linking strategy often depends on the specific domain and the characteristics of the entities you are trying to link.

Implementing advanced entity linking strategies with spaCy often involves a combination of leveraging existing tools and libraries, building custom components, and potentially training machine learning models. The goal is to move beyond simple string matching and use contextual understanding and knowledge graph information to accurately connect entity mentions to their corresponding knowledge base entries.

4.3 Resolving Coreference for Enhanced Understanding

Resolving coreference is a crucial task in Natural Language Processing (NLP) that aims to identify all expressions in a text that refer to the same real-world entity. This is essential for achieving a deeper understanding of the text, as it helps to connect mentions of the same person, place, or object, even when they are expressed using different words or phrases (e.g., pronouns, definite noun phrases).

Here's a breakdown of advanced strategies for coreference resolution, with a focus on how they can be integrated or considered within a spaCy ecosystem:

1. Rule-Based Coreference Resolution:

While often less accurate than machine learning approaches, rule-based systems can be effective for specific types of coreference, especially pronoun resolution in simpler cases. These systems rely on linguistic constraints and heuristics, such as:

Grammatical Agreement: Pronouns should agree in number, gender, and person with their antecedents.

Recency: The most recent plausible antecedent is often the correct one.

Syntactic Constraints: Certain syntactic structures can prevent coreference (e.g., a pronoun within a noun phrase cannot refer to the noun phrase itself).

Semantic Compatibility: The antecedent should be semantically compatible with the pronoun (e.g., "it" usually refers to an inanimate object).

You can implement rule-based coreference within a custom spaCy component by:

Accessing Syntactic Information: Utilize spaCy's part-of-speech tags and dependency parses to analyze the grammatical structure of sentences.

Identifying Pronouns and Noun Phrases: Locate potential referring expressions and their candidates.

Applying Heuristic Rules: Implement the linguistic constraints mentioned above to link pronouns to their antecedents.

Storing Coreference Links: Add custom attributes to spaCy Token or Span objects to store the coreference links (e.g., pointing a pronoun back to its antecedent).

Example (Conceptual Rule-Based):

Python

```python
import spacy
from spacy.language import Language
from spacy.tokens import Doc, Token

@Language.factory("simple_pronoun_resolver")
def create_simple_pronoun_resolver(nlp: Language, name: str):
    def simple_pronoun_resolver(doc: Doc) -> Doc:
        mentions = []
        for token in doc:
            if token.pos_ == "PRON":
```

```python
            mentions.append(token)
        elif token.pos_ in ["NOUN", "PROPN"]:
            mentions.append(token) # Simplify: consider all nouns
as potential antecedents

    resolved = {}
    for pronoun in [m for m in mentions if m.pos_ == "PRON"]:
        # Simple recency and agreement check (very basic)
        for antecedent in reversed([m for m in mentions if m.i <
pronoun.i and m.pos_ in ["NOUN", "PROPN"]]):
            if pronoun.dep_ in ["nsubj", "pobj"] and antecedent.dep_
in ["nsubj", "dobj", "pobj"] and pronoun.morph.get("Number") ==
antecedent.morph.get("Number"):
                resolved[pronoun.i] = antecedent.i
                break
    for token in doc:
        if token.i in resolved:
            token._.coref_antecedent = doc[resolved[token.i]]
    return doc
        Token.set_extension("coref_antecedent", default=None,
force=True)
    return simple_pronoun_resolver

nlp = spacy.load("en_core_web_sm")
nlp.add_pipe("simple_pronoun_resolver")

text = "John went to the store. He bought milk."
doc = nlp(text)
for token in doc:
    print(f"{token.text}: Antecedent = {token._.coref_antecedent}")
```

2. Machine Learning-Based Coreference Resolution:

State-of-the-art coreference resolution relies heavily on machine
learning models that are trained on large annotated corpora (e.g.,

OntoNotes). These models typically learn to identify mentions and then predict whether two mentions refer to the same entity based on various features:

Lexical Features: The words themselves.

Syntactic Features: Part-of-speech tags, dependency relations, syntactic paths.

Semantic Features: Word embeddings, semantic roles.

Discourse Features: Position in the text, topic information.

Mention Pair Features: Distance between mentions, grammatical role of each mention.

Integrating advanced ML-based coreference resolution with spaCy often involves using external libraries that provide pre-trained models:

Hugging Face Transformers: Libraries like `transformers` offer pre-trained coreference resolution models (often based on SpanBERT or similar architectures). You can build a custom spaCy component that takes a `Doc` object, extracts the necessary information, feeds it to the transformer model, and then adds the coreference clusters back to the `Doc` as custom attributes.

AllenNLP: The AllenNLP library also provides sophisticated coreference resolution models. You could potentially integrate these by passing spaCy `Doc` objects or relevant extracted features to AllenNLP's models.

Conceptual Integration with Transformers:

Python

```python
import spacy
from spacy.language import Language
from spacy.tokens import Doc
from transformers import pipeline


@Language.factory("transformer_coref")
def create_transformer_coref(nlp: Language, name: str,
model_name: str = " SpanBERT/spanbert-large-cased"):
    coref_pipeline = pipeline("coreference", model=model_name)
    def transformer_coref(doc: Doc) -> Doc:
        # Need to format the spaCy Doc into a string that the pipeline
expects
        text = doc.text
        clusters = coref_pipeline(text)
        doc._.coref_clusters = clusters # Store raw clusters
        # Further processing needed to link tokens within the Doc
based on clusters
        return doc
    Doc.set_extension("coref_clusters", default=None, force=True)
    return transformer_coref


nlp = spacy.load("en_core_web_sm")
nlp.add_pipe("transformer_coref")


text = "John saw Mary. He waved at her."
doc = nlp(text)
print(doc._.coref_clusters)
# Output will be in the format of the transformer pipeline; further
mapping to spaCy tokens is needed
```

3. Neural Coreference Resolution Models:

These models, often based on neural networks (e.g., LSTMs, Transformers), learn to identify and link mentions end-to-end. They are trained to predict coreference relations directly from the input text and often achieve state-of-the-art results. Integrating them with spaCy follows a similar pattern to using other ML libraries:

Load Pre-trained Models: Utilize pre-trained neural coreference models from libraries like `transformers` or research repositories.

Feature Extraction: Extract relevant features from the spaCy Doc object (tokens, POS tags, dependency parses, embeddings if available).

Inference: Feed these features into the neural coreference model to get coreference predictions (clusters of mentions).

Annotation: Map the predicted coreference clusters back to the spaCy Doc by adding custom attributes to the relevant Token or Span objects.

4. End-to-End Neural Models Integrated with SpaCy:

Ideally, a more seamless integration would involve training or fine-tuning a neural coreference model that directly operates on spaCy's Doc objects or its internal representations. While a fully integrated, trainable end-to-end neural coreference model isn't a standard component in spaCy as of now, future developments or community contributions might bridge this gap.

Challenges and Considerations:

Complexity: Coreference resolution is a complex task, and achieving high accuracy, especially on diverse text, is challenging.

Computational Cost: Advanced neural models can be computationally expensive to run.

Integration Overhead: Integrating external libraries requires careful handling of data formats and mapping results back to spaCy's data structures.

Training Data: Training high-performing coreference models requires large, well-annotated datasets, which can be scarce for specific domains.

Enhancing Understanding with Resolved Coreference:

Once coreference is resolved, you can use this information to enhance downstream NLP tasks:

Improved Information Extraction: By knowing which mentions refer to the same entity, you can aggregate information about that entity across the text.

Better Question Answering: Understanding coreference helps in correctly identifying the entities being referred to in a question and the relevant information in the answer text.

Enhanced Text Summarization: Coreference resolution can help in creating more coherent and less redundant summaries by tracking entities across sentences.

More Accurate Discourse Analysis: Understanding how entities are referred to throughout a text is crucial for analyzing discourse structure and coherence.

In conclusion, resolving coreference for enhanced understanding with spaCy often involves leveraging external, state-of-the-art coreference resolution libraries (primarily those based on machine learning and neural networks) and building custom spaCy components to integrate their predictions with spaCy's linguistic annotations. While rule-based approaches can provide a starting point for simpler cases, achieving high accuracy on complex text requires more sophisticated techniques.

CHAPTER 5

Unlocking the Power of Custom Training

5.1 Preparing and Annotating Data for Advanced Training

Preparing and annotating data for advanced training in spaCy (or any NLP framework) is a critical and often time-consuming process. The quality and format of your data directly impact the performance of your models. For advanced tasks like custom NER, dependency parsing, or relation extraction, meticulous preparation and annotation are even more crucial. Here's a comprehensive breakdown of the steps and considerations:

1. Defining Your Task and Annotation Schema:

Clearly Define the Task: What exactly are you trying to train your model to do? (e.g., identify specific entity types, predict dependency relationships, extract relations between entities).

Develop a Detailed Annotation Schema:

Entities: If it's NER, define all the entity types you want to recognize. Provide clear definitions and examples for each type to ensure annotator consistency. Consider hierarchical or overlapping entities if necessary for your task.

Relations: If it's relation extraction, define the types of relationships you want to identify between entities. Specify the directionality and the roles of the entities involved in each relation.

Dependencies: For dependency parsing, you'll typically use a standard dependency treebank schema for your language (e.g., Universal Dependencies). Ensure your annotators understand these relations.

Other Tasks: For tasks like text classification with explanations, you might need to annotate text spans that justify the classification label.

Create Annotation Guidelines: Document your schema with clear instructions, examples (positive and negative), and edge cases to guide your annotators and ensure consistency.

2. Data Collection and Sampling:

Gather Relevant Data: Collect a corpus of text that is representative of the data your model will encounter in the real world. The source and diversity of your data are important.

Data Sampling Strategy: If you have a large dataset, you might need to sample it for annotation. Ensure your sampling strategy captures the variability and class imbalances present in your data. Consider stratified sampling if certain entity types or relations are rare.

3. Annotation Tools and Setup:

Choose an Annotation Tool: Select a tool that suits your needs and resources. Options include:

Prodigy: A powerful annotation tool from the creators of spaCy, offering active learning capabilities to improve annotation efficiency.

Doccano: An open-source web-based annotation tool that supports various NLP tasks.

Label Studio: Another open-source multi-type data labeling tool.

Custom Scripts: For simpler tasks or specific formats, you might develop your own annotation scripts.

Set Up the Annotation Environment: Ensure your annotators have access to the tool, clear guidelines, and support.

4. The Annotation Process:

Initial Annotation: Annotators go through the data and mark the relevant spans, relations, or dependencies according to the guidelines.

Inter-Annotator Agreement (IAA): To ensure the quality and reliability of your annotations, involve multiple annotators on a subset of the data and measure their agreement (e.g., using Cohen's Kappa or F1-score). Low agreement indicates issues with the schema or guidelines that need to be addressed.

Annotation Review and Refinement: Have experienced annotators or domain experts review and correct the initial annotations. This step helps to catch errors and inconsistencies.

Iterative Refinement: The annotation process is often iterative. Based on IAA scores and review feedback, you might need to refine your schema, guidelines, or even the data itself.

5. Data Conversion to spaCy Format:

SpaCy's training pipeline expects the data in a specific format. You'll need to convert your annotated data into this format:

NER: For Named Entity Recognition, spaCy expects a list of tuples for each document. Each tuple contains the start and end character indices of an entity and its label:

Python

```
[
    ("Patient John Doe presented with fever.", {"entities": [(0, 14,
"PERSON"), (33, 38, "SYMPTOM")]}),
    ("The company Acme Corp reported $1 million revenue.",
{"entities": [(12, 22, "ORG"), (31, 40, "MONEY")]}),
]
```

Dependency Parsing and Other Tasks: For dependency parsing, text classification with explanations, and other advanced tasks, the format might be more complex and involve creating Doc objects with specific annotations. SpaCy's Example class is often used to represent training examples for various tasks.

Python

```
from spacy.training import Example
from spacy.tokens import Doc

# For dependency parsing (simplified)
```

```python
def create_dep_example(nlp, text, heads, deps):
    doc = nlp.make_doc(text)
    example = Example.from_dict(doc, {"heads": heads, "deps": deps})
    return example

nlp = spacy.blank("en")
text = "The cat sat on the mat ."
heads = [2, 0, 2, 4, 2, 4] # Indices of head words
deps = ["DET", "ROOT", "NSUBJ", "ADP", "DET", "POBJ", "PUNCT"]
dep_example = create_dep_example(nlp, text, heads, deps)
```

Relation Extraction: For relation extraction, you'll typically need to annotate entities and the relations between them, often represented as tuples of (head entity, relation type, tail entity) along with the text. You'll then need to convert this into a format that spaCy's custom components or training scripts can understand. This might involve creating custom data structures or extending spaCy's Doc object with relation annotations.

Saving in `.spacy` **Format:** For efficient training, it's recommended to convert your training and development data into spaCy's binary `.spacy` format using the `DocBin` class:

Python

```python
import spacy
from spacy.tokens import DocBin
```

```python
def save_to_spacy_bin(data, output_path, nlp):
    db = DocBin()
    for text, annotations in data:
        doc = nlp.make_doc(text)
        ents = []
        for start, end, label in annotations.get("entities", []):
            span = doc.char_span(start, end, label=label)
            if span is not None:
                ents.append(span)
        doc.ents = ents
        db.add(doc)
    db.to_disk(output_path)

nlp = spacy.blank("en") # Or load your base model's vocabulary
TRAIN_DATA = [("...", {"entities": [...]}), ...]
save_to_spacy_bin(TRAIN_DATA, "train.spacy", nlp)
```

6. Data Augmentation (Optional but Recommended for Advanced Training):

To improve the robustness and generalization of your models, especially with limited data, consider data augmentation techniques:

Random Word Deletion/Insertion/Substitution: Introduce minor variations in the text while preserving the meaning and entity context.

Synonym Replacement: Replace words with their synonyms.

Back Translation: Translate the text to another language and back to introduce variations.

Contextual Augmentation: Use language models to suggest plausible variations in the context of entities.

For structured tasks like dependency parsing, you might augment by syntactically transforming sentences while preserving the dependencies.

Implement data augmentation carefully to ensure that the annotations remain valid after the transformations.

7. Data Splitting:

Divide your prepared and annotated data into training, development (validation), and test sets. The development set is used during training to monitor performance and tune hyperparameters. The test set is used only at the very end to evaluate the final model's performance on unseen data. A typical split might be 70-80% training, 10-15% development, and 10-15% test.

Key Considerations for Advanced Training Data:

Data Quality over Quantity: While more data can be helpful, high-quality, consistently annotated data is more important for achieving good performance.

Representativeness: Ensure your training data accurately reflects the variety of text your model will encounter in deployment.

Balance: If your task involves classifying entities or relations, try to have a balanced distribution of classes in your training data to avoid bias.

Handling Overlapping Annotations: For tasks like NER or relation extraction, you might encounter overlapping entities or relations. Your annotation schema and training process need to handle these cases appropriately.

Negative Samples: For relation extraction and some other tasks, you might need to explicitly include negative samples (examples where a relation does not exist between two entities).

Documentation: Keep thorough documentation of your annotation schema, guidelines, and the data preparation process.

By following these steps and paying close attention to detail, you can prepare and annotate high-quality data that will enable you to train effective and robust advanced NLP models with spaCy. Remember that this is an iterative process, and you might need to revisit earlier steps as you gain more insights into your data and task.

5.2 Implementing Effective Training Loops and Strategies

Implementing effective training loops and strategies is crucial for successfully training advanced spaCy models. A well-designed training loop ensures that your model learns from the data in a controlled manner, while appropriate strategies help to optimize performance, prevent overfitting, and handle various training challenges. Here's a breakdown of key aspects:

1. The Basic Training Loop:

At its core, a training loop involves iterating over your training data multiple times (epochs) and updating the model's parameters based on the gradients calculated from the loss function. A typical loop looks like this:

Python

```python
import spacy
import random
from spacy.training import Example

def train(nlp, train_data, optimizer, n_iter=30):
    losses = {}
    for i in range(n_iter):
        random.shuffle(train_data)
        for batch in spacy.util.minibatch(train_data, size=8): # Adjust batch size
            examples = [Example.from_dict(nlp.make_doc(text), annotations) for text, annotations in batch]
            nlp.update(examples, sgd=optimizer, losses=losses)
        print(f"Epoch {i+1} Loss: {losses}")
    return nlp
```

This is a simplified example. Real-world training loops often include more sophisticated elements.

2. Key Components of an Effective Training Loop:

Data Loading and Batching: Efficiently load your training data and divide it into smaller batches. SpaCy's `spacy.util.minibatch` is a helpful utility for this. The batch size can significantly impact training stability and speed. Experiment with different sizes.

Forward Pass: For each batch, pass the input through the model to get predictions.

Loss Calculation: Compare the model's predictions with the gold annotations to calculate the loss. The choice of loss function depends on the task (e.g., categorical cross-entropy for classification, softmax loss for NER). SpaCy handles this internally within the `nlp.update()` method for its built-in components.

Gradient Calculation: Compute the gradients of the loss with respect to the model's parameters using backpropagation. SpaCy handles this automatically.

Parameter Update: Adjust the model's parameters based on the calculated gradients and the optimizer algorithm. SpaCy's `nlp.update()` takes an `optimizer` argument (usually an instance of `spacy.util.Adam`).

Evaluation: Periodically evaluate the model's performance on a development/validation set to monitor progress and detect overfitting. This is crucial for knowing when to stop training or adjust hyperparameters.

3. Advanced Training Strategies:

Learning Rate Scheduling: The learning rate controls the step size during parameter updates. A fixed learning rate might not be optimal throughout training. Learning rate scheduling involves adjusting the learning rate over time. Common strategies include:

Decay: Gradually reduce the learning rate (e.g., step decay, exponential decay).

Cyclical Learning Rates: Vary the learning rate between bounds.

Adaptive Learning Rates (handled by optimizers like Adam): Optimizers like Adam automatically adjust the learning rate for each parameter based on the gradients. You can still tune the initial learning rate for Adam.

Gradient Clipping: To prevent exploding gradients (where gradients become very large, leading to unstable training), you can clip the gradients to a certain threshold. SpaCy's `nlp.update()` method has a `clip` argument for this.

Dropout: A regularization technique that randomly sets a fraction of the neuron outputs to zero during training. This helps prevent overfitting. Dropout rates are typically configured within the model architecture in your `config.cfg` file.

Early Stopping: Monitor the performance on the validation set and stop training when the performance plateaus or starts to degrade, even if you haven't reached the maximum number of epochs. This helps prevent overfitting. You'll need to implement this logic in your training script.

Weight Decay (L2 Regularization): Adds a penalty to the loss function based on the magnitude of the model's weights, encouraging smaller weights and preventing overfitting. This is often configured within the optimizer.

Transfer Learning and Fine-Tuning: As discussed earlier, starting with a pre-trained model and fine-tuning it on your domain-specific data is a powerful strategy, especially when you have limited annotated data. You can control which layers are fine-tuned and the learning rates used for different parts of the model.

Multi-Task Learning: If your data allows, you can train a single model to perform multiple related tasks simultaneously (e.g., NER and POS tagging). This can improve performance on individual tasks by leveraging shared representations. SpaCy's configuration allows for multi-task pipelines.

Active Learning: An iterative process where the model is trained on a small initial set of data, then used to predict on unlabeled data. The most uncertain or informative examples are then manually annotated and added to the training set, and the model is retrained. This can significantly reduce the amount of data needed for good performance. Prodigy is a tool that facilitates active learning with spaCy.

Ensemble Methods: Train multiple independent models and combine their predictions to improve robustness and accuracy.

Handling Class Imbalance: If your data has imbalanced classes (e.g., some entity types are much more frequent than others), you might need strategies like:

Weighted Loss Functions: Assign higher weights to the loss for minority classes.

Oversampling/Undersampling: Adjust the number of samples for different classes in your training batches.

Checkpointing and Model Saving: Regularly save the state of your model during training so you can resume training if it's interrupted or revert to a previous, better-performing version. SpaCy's `spacy train` command handles saving automatically.

4. Implementing Evaluation During Training:

It's crucial to evaluate your model on a separate development set at the end of each epoch (or at regular intervals) to track progress and detect overfitting. This involves:

Python

```python
from spacy.scorer import Scorer
from spacy.training import Example

def evaluate(nlp, dev_data):
    scorer = Scorer()
    examples = [Example.from_dict(nlp.make_doc(text),
annotations) for text, annotations in dev_data]
    scores = nlp.evaluate(examples) # More integrated way in
recent spaCy versions
    print(f"Evaluation Scores: {scores}")
    return scores["ents_f"] # Example: Return NER F-score

def train_with_evaluation(nlp, train_data, dev_data, optimizer,
n_iter=30):
    best_f1 = 0.0
    for i in range(n_iter):
        # Training loop as before
        # ...
        eval_scores = evaluate(nlp, dev_data)
        if eval_scores > best_f1:
            best_f1 = eval_scores
            # Save the current best model
            nlp.to_disk(f"./model_epoch_{i+1}")
    print(f"Best F1 on dev set: {best_f1}")
    return nlp
```

5. Using SpaCy's Built-in Training:

SpaCy's `spacy train` command in the terminal provides a robust and well-structured way to train models using a configuration file (`config.cfg`). This method handles many of the effective training strategies mentioned above (e.g., learning rate scheduling, gradient clipping, evaluation) and is the recommended approach for most users. You configure these strategies within the `[training]` and `[optimizer]` sections of your `config.cfg`.

Key Takeaways for Effective Training:

Understand your data and task thoroughly.

Choose appropriate evaluation metrics.

Monitor performance on a separate development set.

Experiment with different hyperparameters and training strategies.

Leverage spaCy's built-in training capabilities and configuration options.

Consider using tools like TensorBoard or Weights & Biases to visualize training progress and metrics.

By carefully designing your training loop and employing effective training strategies, you can significantly improve the performance and generalization ability of your advanced spaCy models.

5.3 Evaluating and Iterating on Custom Models

Evaluating and iterating on custom spaCy models is a crucial part of the development process. It allows you to understand how well your model is performing, identify areas for improvement, and ultimately deploy a robust and accurate NLP solution. Here's a detailed guide on how to approach this:

1. Setting Up Evaluation Metrics:

The first step is to define the metrics that are relevant to your specific task. SpaCy provides built-in evaluation capabilities and metrics for various components:

NER (Named Entity Recognition): Precision, recall, F1-score (for each entity type and overall), and potentially per-entity accuracy.

Dependency Parsing: Unlabeled Attachment Score (UAS), Labeled Attachment Score (LAS).

Text Classification: Accuracy, precision, recall, F1-score (per class and macro/micro averages), AUC.

Tokenization and Sentence Segmentation: Accuracy of token boundaries and sentence boundaries.

Custom Components: You'll need to define metrics that are specific to the task your custom component performs.

SpaCy's `Scorer` class and the `nlp.evaluate()` method are key tools for calculating these metrics.

2. Creating a Representative Evaluation Dataset:

Your evaluation should be performed on a held-out dataset (the test set) that the model has never seen during training or development. This dataset should be representative of the real-world data your model will encounter. Ensure that the class distribution and the types of examples in your evaluation set are similar to your production data.

3. Performing Initial Evaluation:

After training your custom model (or a specific iteration during training), evaluate it on your test set using `nlp.evaluate()`. This method takes a list of `Example` objects (containing the text and the gold annotations) and returns a dictionary of evaluation scores.

Python

```python
import spacy
from spacy.training import Example

def evaluate_model(nlp, test_data):
    examples = []
    for text, annotations in test_data:
        doc = nlp(text)
        example = Example.from_dict(doc, annotations)
        examples.append(example)
    scores = nlp.evaluate(examples)
    return scores

# Load your trained model
trained_nlp = spacy.load("./output/model-best")
TEST_DATA = [("...", {"entities": [...]}), ...] # Your test data
test_scores = evaluate_model(trained_nlp, TEST_DATA)
print(test_scores)
```

4. Analyzing Evaluation Results:

Carefully examine the evaluation scores. Pay attention to:

Overall Performance: How well is the model performing on the primary metrics (e.g., overall F1-score for NER, UAS/LAS for parsing, accuracy for classification)?

Per-Class Performance: Look at the precision, recall, and F1-score for each entity type or class. This can reveal if the model is struggling with specific categories.

Common Errors: Analyze the types of errors the model is making. For NER, are there false positives (predicting an entity where there isn't one), false negatives (missing an entity), or incorrect entity types? For parsing, are there systematic errors in attaching certain types of dependencies?

5. Error Analysis and Debugging:

To gain deeper insights, perform manual error analysis:

Visualize Predictions: For dependency parsing, visualize the predicted dependency trees and compare them to the gold trees. Tools like displaCy can be helpful.

Inspect Misclassified Examples: Look at specific examples where the model made incorrect predictions. Identify patterns in these errors.

Consider Edge Cases: Test your model on challenging or ambiguous examples to see how it handles them.

Analyze Confusion Matrices (for classification and NER): These matrices show the counts of true positives, true negatives, false positives, and false negatives for each class, providing a detailed view of where the model is making mistakes.

6. Iteration and Model Improvement:

Based on your evaluation and error analysis, iterate on your model and training process. Potential areas for improvement include:

Data Augmentation: Increase the size and diversity of your training data by applying data augmentation techniques.

Improving Annotation Quality: If you identify inconsistencies or errors in your annotations, refine your annotation guidelines and re-annotate a subset of your data.

Adjusting Training Parameters: Experiment with different learning rates, batch sizes, dropout rates, and the number of training epochs.

Modifying the Model Architecture: For advanced users, you might consider experimenting with different model architectures or adding custom layers.

Feature Engineering (if applicable): For some tasks, you might be able to engineer additional features that provide the model with more relevant information.

Addressing Class Imbalance: If you observed poor performance on minority classes, apply techniques to handle class imbalance.

Refining Preprocessing Steps: Ensure your text preprocessing is appropriate for your task and data.

Adding or Modifying Pipeline Components: Depending on the errors, you might need to adjust your spaCy pipeline (e.g., add a custom component for rule-based correction).

7. Tracking Experiments and Results:

Keep track of the different experiments you run, the changes you make, and the corresponding evaluation results. Tools like MLflow, TensorBoard, or even a simple spreadsheet can help you manage this information and identify what changes lead to improvements.

8. Statistical Significance (for rigorous evaluation):

If you are comparing different models or significant changes, consider performing statistical significance tests on your evaluation metrics to determine if the observed differences are statistically meaningful or simply due to random variation.

9. Deployment Considerations:

Once you are satisfied with your model's performance on the evaluation set, consider the practical aspects of deployment:

Speed and Efficiency: Evaluate the model's inference speed and resource usage. You might need to optimize the model for deployment (e.g., using smaller models or quantization).

Robustness: Test the model on a variety of real-world inputs to ensure it is robust to different styles and potential noise.

Monitoring: Plan for monitoring the model's performance in production and having a process for retraining if its accuracy degrades over time.

In summary, evaluating and iterating on custom spaCy models is a cyclical process:

1.Evaluate: Measure performance on a representative test set using relevant metrics.

2. Analyze: Understand the types of errors the model is making.

3. Iterate: Make informed changes to your data, training process, or model based on the error analysis.

4. Repeat: Continue evaluating and iterating until you achieve satisfactory performance.

This systematic approach is essential for building high-quality custom NLP models with spaCy. Remember that the specific steps and techniques will vary depending on the complexity of your task and the characteristics of your data.

CHAPTER 6

Leveraging Transformers with spaCy

6.1 Integrating Transformer Models for Enhanced Accuracy

Integrating transformer models into spaCy can significantly enhance the accuracy of your NLP pipelines, especially for tasks like NER, text classification, and dependency parsing. Transformer models, such as BERT, RoBERTa, and DistilBERT, capture contextual information more effectively than traditional statistical models. Here's how to integrate them and key considerations:

1. Using the `spacy-transformers` **Library:**

The `spacy-transformers` library provides a bridge between spaCy and Hugging Face's `transformers` library, allowing you to incorporate pre-trained transformer models into your spaCy pipelines.

Installation: Install both libraries:

Bash

```
pip install spacy-transformers
```

Choosing a Model: Select a suitable pre-trained transformer model from Hugging Face's Model Hub (https://huggingface.co/models). Consider factors like model size, language, task-specific fine-tuning, and computational resources.

Configuration: Modify your spaCy configuration file (`config.cfg`) to include the transformer component. This typically involves:

Specifying the transformer model name in the `[components.transformer]` section.

Adjusting the pipeline to include the `transformer` component and potentially modifying downstream components to work with the transformer's output.

Setting appropriate batch sizes and gradient accumulation steps for efficient training.

2. Example Configuration (simplified):

Ini, TOML

```
[components]
transformer = {factory = "transformer", model_name = "bert-base-uncased"}
ner = {factory = "ner"} # Or other downstream component

[pipeline]
- "transformer"
- "ner"

[training]
```

```
batch_size = 16
```

3. Code Example (Training with Transformers):

Python

```python
import spacy

# Create or load a spaCy model with the transformer in the
pipeline
nlp = spacy.load("en_core_web_trf")   # Or create a custom
pipeline from config

# Prepare your training data (as before)
TRAIN_DATA = [
    ("Apple is looking at buying U.K. startup for $1 billion",
{"entities": [(0, 5, "ORG")]}),
    ("Google announced a new AI model.", {"entities": [(0, 6,
"ORG")]}),
]

# Start or resume training
nlp.begin_training()
for i in range(10):  # Example epochs
    for batch in spacy.util.minibatch(TRAIN_DATA, size=2):
        for text, annotations in batch:
            doc = nlp.make_doc(text)
            example = spacy.training.Example.from_dict(doc,
annotations)
        nlp.update([example], drop=0.2) # Example dropout
    nlp.evaluate(TRAIN_DATA) # Evaluate on training data for
demonstration
    nlp.to_disk(f"model_epoch_{i}") # Save model
```

4. Key Considerations:

Subword Tokenization: Transformer models use subword tokenization (e.g., WordPiece, SentencePiece). `spacy-transformers` handles this automatically, aligning spaCy's tokens with the transformer's subword tokens. You typically don't need to implement custom tokenization.

Pipeline Adjustments: Downstream components (e.g., NER, parser) need to be adapted to work with the output of the transformer model (which is typically a tensor representing contextualized word embeddings). `spacy-transformers` provides default architectures that work well in many cases.

Computational Resources: Transformer models are computationally intensive. Training and inference can be slow, especially for larger models. Consider using a GPU.

Memory Usage: Transformer models can consume a significant amount of memory. Optimize your batch sizes and use gradient accumulation to manage memory usage.

Fine-Tuning: Fine-tuning the transformer model on your task-specific data is crucial for achieving optimal performance.

Model Selection: Choose a pre-trained model that is appropriate for your language and task. Some models are fine-tuned for specific tasks (e.g., NER).

Configuration Complexity: `spacy-transformers` configuration can be complex. Start with example configurations and adjust them carefully.

5. Alternatives (Less Common):

While `spacy-transformers` is the recommended approach, you could technically:

Extract Transformer Embeddings Manually: Use the `transformers` library directly to get embeddings and then feed them into a custom spaCy component. This is less efficient and requires more manual handling.

Build a Completely Custom Component: Create a spaCy component that directly wraps a transformer model, but this is a complex undertaking.

By integrating transformer models using `spacy-transformers`, you can significantly improve the accuracy of your spaCy pipelines for a wide range of NLP tasks. Remember to carefully select and configure your model and to fine-tune it on your specific data for best results.

6.2 Fine-Tuning Transformer Architectures within spaCy

Fine-tuning transformer architectures within spaCy, primarily through the `spacy-transformers` library, allows you to adapt powerful pre-trained models to your specific NLP tasks and datasets. This process leverages the contextual understanding of transformers while optimizing them for your particular needs. Here's a breakdown of how to approach this:

1. Understanding the Configuration:

The key to fine-tuning transformer architectures in `spacy-transformers` lies in the `config.cfg` file. This file defines the entire training setup, including the model architecture, data paths, training parameters, and pipeline components. When using transformers, you'll be particularly interested in the `[components.transformer.model]` section.

`@architectures`: This key specifies the architecture to use. `spacy-transformers` provides several built-in architectures that wrap models from the `transformers` library. Examples include:

`spacy-transformers.TransformerModel.v2`: A general-purpose transformer wrapper.

`spacy-transformers.BertModel.v2`: Specifically for BERT-like models.

`spacy-transformers.RobertaModel.v2`: Specifically for RoBERTa-like models.

And others for different transformer families.

`name`: This parameter within the architecture specifies the pre-trained transformer model name from Hugging Face's Model Hub (e.g., `bert-base-uncased`, `roberta-large`, `distilbert-base-uncased`). This is the foundational model you'll be fine-tuning.

`config`: This subsection allows you to pass specific configuration parameters directly to the underlying transformer model's `from_pretrained()` method. This can include things like:

`hidden_dropout_prob`: Dropout rate for hidden layers.

`attention_probs_dropout_prob`: Dropout rate for attention probabilities.[1]

`num_hidden_layers`: Number of hidden layers to use (though generally, you'd fine-tune the entire pre-trained architecture).

`gradient_checkpointing`: A technique to reduce memory usage during training by recomputing gradients instead of storing all intermediate activations. Can be beneficial for large models.

`pooling`: Specifies how to pool the output of the transformer model to get a representation for each spaCy token. Common options include `mean`, `max`, or using the CLS token. The choice can impact downstream task performance.

2. Fine-Tuning Strategies:

Full Fine-Tuning: By default, when you train a spaCy pipeline with a transformer, all the layers of the pre-trained transformer model are trainable. This allows the model to fully adapt to your specific task and data. However, it requires a significant amount of task-specific data and computational resources.

Layer Freezing (Selective Fine-Tuning): If you have limited data or want to prevent catastrophic forgetting of the pre-trained knowledge, you can freeze some of the earlier layers of the transformer and only train the later layers or the layers connected to the task-specific heads (e.g., the classification layer on top). You can control which layers are trainable by:

Customizing the Architecture: While `spacy-transformers` doesn't offer explicit layer freezing in the config, you could potentially create a custom architecture that loads the pre-trained model and then sets `requires_grad = False` for specific layers before passing it to the downstream task layers. This requires more advanced PyTorch knowledge.

Lower Learning Rates for Earlier Layers: A more common approach is to use a lower learning rate for the earlier layers of the transformer and a higher learning rate for the later layers and task-specific heads. This allows the earlier layers to make smaller adjustments while the later layers adapt more quickly to the new task. You can implement this using custom optimizers or by manipulating parameter groups in your training script (if you're writing a custom training loop).

Adapter Layers: Adapter layers are small, lightweight neural network modules that are inserted into the transformer architecture. During fine-tuning, only these adapter layers are trained, while the original transformer weights are kept frozen. This is a parameter-efficient way to adapt large pre-trained models to new tasks with limited data. While `spacy-transformers` doesn't have built-in support for adapter layers, you might explore external libraries that implement them and integrate them into a custom architecture.

Prompt Tuning: Instead of directly fine-tuning the transformer's weights, prompt tuning involves learning soft prompts (sequences of embedding vectors) that are prepended to the input text. The pre-trained transformer's language modeling capabilities are then leveraged to generate task-specific outputs based on these prompts. This is a very parameter-efficient approach. Integration with `spacy-transformers` would likely require a custom component and careful handling of the input format.

3. Implementing Fine-Tuning in `config.cfg`:

For standard full fine-tuning or adjusting basic transformer parameters, you primarily work within the `config.cfg`.

Ini, TOML

```
[components]
transformer = {factory = "transformer", model_name = "bert-large-uncased"}
ner = {factory = "ner"}

[pipeline]
- "transformer"
- "ner"

[components.transformer.model]
@architectures = "spacy-transformers.TransformerModel.v2"
name = ${components.transformer.model.model_name}
config = {"hidden_dropout_prob": 0.1, "attention_probs_dropout_prob": 0.1}
pooling = {"@layers": "spacy-transformers.util.mean_pooling.v1"}

[training]
# ...
optimizer = {"@optimizers": "Adam.v1", "learn_rate": 1e-5} # Potentially a lower learning rate for fine-tuning
```

4. Advanced Fine-Tuning with Custom Code:

For more advanced techniques like layer freezing with differential learning rates or integrating adapter layers, you'll likely need to write custom training loops or modify the model loading and parameter updating steps within your Python training scripts. This would involve:

Loading the Pre-trained Model: Use the `transformers` library to load the model.

Accessing Layers: Inspect the model's named parameters to identify specific layers.

Freezing Layers: Set `requires_grad = False` for the parameters of the layers you want to freeze.

Defining Parameter Groups for the Optimizer: Create separate parameter groups for different parts of the model and assign different learning rates to each group.

Using a Custom Training Loop: Instead of relying solely on `nlp.begin_training()` and `nlp.update()`, you might need to implement a more granular training loop using PyTorch's `optimizer.step()` and gradient management.

5. Monitoring and Evaluation:

During fine-tuning, it's crucial to monitor the performance on your development set. Pay attention to metrics relevant to your task. You might observe that fine-tuning a large transformer requires careful tuning of the learning rate and other hyperparameters. Tools like TensorBoard or Weights & Biases can help visualize the training progress and identify the best hyperparameter settings.

Key Considerations for Fine-Tuning Transformers:

Data Size: Fine-tuning large transformers effectively often requires a substantial amount of task-specific data. With limited data, more aggressive regularization or selective fine-tuning might be necessary.

Computational Resources: Fine-tuning large models can be very computationally expensive and time-consuming. GPUs are essential.

Hyperparameter Tuning: The learning rate, batch size, and number of training epochs are critical hyperparameters to tune. Lower learning rates are often used for fine-tuning compared to training from scratch.

Overfitting: Large models are prone to overfitting, especially with limited data. Use techniques like dropout, weight decay, and early stopping.

Task Similarity: The more similar your target task is to the pre-training tasks of the transformer (e.g., masked language modeling), the less data and fine-tuning might be required.

Fine-tuning transformer architectures within spaCy offers a powerful way to achieve state-of-the-art results on various NLP tasks. By carefully configuring the `config.cfg` and potentially writing custom training code for advanced strategies, you can effectively adapt these models to your specific domain and requirements.

6.3 Building Hybrid spaCy Pipelines with Transformers

Building hybrid spaCy pipelines with transformers involves combining the strengths of traditional spaCy components with the powerful contextual embeddings from transformer models. This allows you to leverage spaCy's efficient and well-structured NLP processing while boosting accuracy on tasks that benefit from deep contextual understanding. Here's a breakdown of how to create such pipelines and key considerations:

1. Core Idea: Integrating Transformer Embeddings:

The fundamental concept is to use a transformer model to generate rich, contextualized word embeddings for your text and then feed these embeddings into downstream spaCy components (e.g., a statistical NER model, a dependency parser). The `spacy-transformers` library is the primary tool for this integration.

2. Pipeline Structure:

A typical hybrid pipeline will include:

`transformer` **component (from** `spacy-transformers`**):** This component takes the raw text as input, tokenizes it using the transformer's tokenizer (which might be subword-based), passes it through the transformer model to get contextual embeddings, and stores these embeddings in the `Doc` object.

Traditional spaCy components: These components (e.g., `ner`, `parser`, `tagger`) are configured to use the transformer embeddings instead of (or in addition to) spaCy's traditional token features. `spacy-transformers` often provides custom architectures for these components that are designed to work with transformer outputs.

3. Configuration (`config.cfg`):

The `config.cfg` file is where you define this hybrid pipeline. Here's a simplified example:

Ini, TOML

```
[components]
transformer = {factory = "transformer", model_name = "bert-base-uncased"}
```

```
ner = {factory = "ner"}

[pipeline]
- "transformer"
- "ner"

[components.ner]
# Configuration for the NER component to use transformer
embeddings
model = {"@architectures": "spacy-transformers.NER.v1", "nO":
null}
```

In this configuration:

We include a `transformer` component that loads the `bert-base-uncased` model.

We have a standard `ner` component.

The `pipeline` specifies the order of execution: first the transformer, then the NER model.

The `[components.ner.model]` section typically specifies a model architecture (`spacy-transformers.NER.v1` is a common one) that knows how to utilize the transformer embeddings stored in the `Doc`.

4. Training:

When you train a spaCy model with this configuration, the `transformer` component will process the text and add the transformer outputs to the `Doc`. The subsequent components (like `ner`) will then use these features during training to learn to make predictions. This effectively fine-tunes the downstream spaCy components to leverage the contextual information from the transformer.

5. Advanced Hybrid Strategies:

Feature Augmentation: You can configure spaCy components to use *both* traditional spaCy features (e.g., POS tags, morphological features) and transformer embeddings. This can sometimes lead to better performance, especially when the traditional features provide complementary information.

Multi-Task Learning with Transformers: You can have a single transformer backbone feeding into multiple spaCy components for different tasks (e.g., NER and dependency parsing). This can improve efficiency and potentially boost performance through shared representations. You would define multiple components in your pipeline that consume the transformer output.

Custom Architectures: For more fine-grained control, you can define custom model architectures within your `config.cfg` that specify exactly how the transformer embeddings are used by the downstream components. This might involve adding custom layers or combining the embeddings with other features in specific ways.

Freezing Transformer Layers: As discussed in the fine-tuning section, you can freeze some or all of the transformer's layers during training if you have limited task-specific data or want to prevent catastrophic forgetting. This is configured within the `config.cfg` or through custom training scripts.

Using Different Transformer Layers: You can choose to use the embeddings from different layers of the transformer model (e.g., the last layer, a concatenation of several layers) as input to your spaCy components. This can be configured in the `[components.transformer.model.pooling]` section or within custom architectures.

6. Benefits of Hybrid Pipelines:

Enhanced Accuracy: Transformer models provide rich contextual embeddings, leading to significant improvements in accuracy for many NLP tasks compared to models relying solely on traditional word embeddings and statistical features.

Leveraging SpaCy's Ecosystem: You can still use spaCy's efficient data structures, training pipeline, evaluation framework, and deployment capabilities.

Flexibility: You can combine different transformer models with various spaCy components and architectures to tailor your pipeline to your specific needs.

7. Considerations:

Computational Cost: Pipelines with transformers are generally more computationally expensive (both in terms of training time and inference speed) than traditional spaCy pipelines.**Memory Usage:** Transformer models can have a large memory footprint. Optimize batch sizes and consider techniques like gradient accumulation.

Configuration Complexity: Setting up and tuning `spacy-transformers` configurations can be more complex than configuring traditional spaCy pipelines.

Dependency on `spacy-transformers`: Your pipeline will depend on this external library.

8. Example (Conceptual - Feature Augmentation):

You might have a custom NER architecture that concatenates the transformer embeddings with spaCy's built-in token features before feeding them into a classification layer. This would be defined in the `[components.ner.model]` section of your `config.cfg` using spaCy's architecture registry.

Building hybrid spaCy pipelines with transformers is a powerful way to achieve state-of-the-art performance on various NLP tasks while still benefiting from spaCy's strengths. The `spacy-transformers` library makes this integration relatively seamless, allowing you to leverage the power of pre-trained language models within the familiar spaCy framework. Remember to carefully configure your pipeline and fine-tune it on your specific data for optimal results.

CHAPTER 7

Advanced Text Classification and Categorization

7.1 Implementing Hierarchical and Multi-Label Classification

Implementing hierarchical and multi-label text classification with spaCy requires a more involved approach than standard single-label classification. SpaCy's built-in `TextCategorizer` component is primarily designed for single-label or independent multi-label classification. For hierarchical and true multi-label scenarios (where labels are not independent), you'll often need to extend its functionality or build custom components. Here's a breakdown of the strategies:

1. Understanding Hierarchical and Multi-Label Classification:

Hierarchical Classification: Categories are organized in a tree-like structure. Predicting a category at a lower level implies membership in its parent category. For example, a document classified as "Fiction/Science Fiction/Space Opera" is also implicitly classified as "Fiction" and "Fiction/Science Fiction."

Multi-Label Classification: Each document can belong to multiple categories simultaneously, and these categories might or might not be related. For example, a news article could be tagged with "Politics," "International Relations," and "Europe."

2. Strategies for Implementation with spaCy:

a) Independent Multi-Label Classification (Using `TextCategorizer`):

If your multi-labels are largely independent, you can train a `TextCategorizer` with multiple output heads (one for each label). SpaCy's configuration allows you to define multiple exclusive or non-exclusive classes.

Ini, TOML

```
[components]
textcat = {factory = "text_categorizer"}

[pipeline]
- "textcat"

[components.textcat]
model = {
    "@architectures" = "spacy.TextCatBOW.v2",
    "exclusive_classes" = false, # Set to false for multi-label
    "ngram_size" = 1,
    "no_output_layer" = false
}
scorer = {"@scorers" = "spacy.scorer.threshold_scorer.v1"}
threshold = 0.5 # Adjust threshold for assigning labels
```

In your training data, the `annotations` for each text would be a dictionary where the keys are your labels and the values are booleans (True if the label applies, False otherwise).

Python

```
TRAIN_DATA = [
    ("This is about politics and international relations.", {"cats":
{"POLITICS": True, "INTERNATIONAL_RELATIONS": True,
"SCIENCE": False}}),
```

```
("A new study in physics was published.", {"cats": {"POLITICS":
False,   "INTERNATIONAL_RELATIONS":   False,   "SCIENCE":
True}}),
  # ...
]
```

Limitations: This approach treats each label independently and doesn't inherently capture hierarchical relationships or dependencies between labels.

b) Custom Components for Hierarchical Classification:

To handle hierarchical structures, you'll likely need to build a custom spaCy component that implements a strategy for predicting labels at different levels of the hierarchy. Some approaches include:

Level-by-Level   Classification: Train   a   separate
`TextCategorizer` (or a custom model) for each level of the hierarchy. The output of a higher-level classifier can be used as input or to constrain the predictions of lower-level classifiers.

Single Model with Hierarchical Output: Design a custom neural network architecture that has an output layer reflecting the hierarchical structure. For example, you could have a shared base network followed by branches for each level of the hierarchy, with constraints on the predictions (e.g., if the parent node is not predicted, the child nodes cannot be).

Using External Libraries: Integrate libraries specifically designed for hierarchical classification (though direct spaCy integration might require custom components).

Example (Conceptual Level-by-Level):

Python

```python
import spacy
from spacy.language import Language
from spacy.tokens import Doc
from spacy.training import Example


@Language.factory("hierarchical_classifier")
class HierarchicalClassifier:
    def __init__(self, nlp, name, level1_model_path,
level2_model_path):
        self.level1_nlp = spacy.load(level1_model_path)
        self.level2_nlp = spacy.load(level2_model_path) # Assuming
model per top-level category

    def __call__(self, doc: Doc) -> Doc:
        level1_doc = self.level1_nlp(doc.text)
        level1_label = max(level1_doc.cats, key=level1_doc.cats.get)
if level1_doc.cats else None

        doc._.hierarchical_labels = {"level1": level1_label, "level2":
None}

        if level1_label and level1_label in self.level2_nlp.pipe_names:
            level2_doc = self.level2_nlp(doc.text)
            level2_label = max(level2_doc.cats,
key=level2_doc.cats.get) if level2_doc.cats else None
            doc._.hierarchical_labels["level2"] =
f"{level1_label}/{level2_label}"

        return doc

Language.factory("hierarchical_classifier",
func=HierarchicalClassifier)
```

```
# Training would involve training separate models for each
level/category
# nlp = spacy.load("en_core_web_sm")
#                              nlp.add_pipe("hierarchical_classifier",
config={"level1_model_path": ..., "level2_model_path": ...})
```

c) Custom Components for True Multi-Label Classification with Dependencies:

When labels have dependencies, you might need a model that can learn these relationships. This often involves custom neural network architectures:

Using Embeddings and Relationships: Train embeddings for the labels themselves and model the relationships between them. The prediction of one label can influence the prediction of others.

Graph Neural Networks (GNNs): If the label space has a known graph structure, GNNs can be used to propagate information between related labels.

Transformer-Based Models: Fine-tuning transformer models with a multi-label classification head can sometimes capture label dependencies implicitly through the attention mechanism.

You would implement such models as custom PyTorch or TensorFlow layers within a custom spaCy component. The training loop would also need to be adapted to handle the multi-label data and the custom loss function.

Example (Conceptual Custom Component with PyTorch):

Python

```
import spacy
from spacy.language import Language
```

```python
from spacy.tokens import Doc
import torch
import torch.nn as nn
import torch.optim as optim


class MultiLabelModel(nn.Module):
    def __init__(self, n_input, n_labels):
        super().__init__()
        self.linear = nn.Linear(n_input, n_labels)
        self.sigmoid = nn.Sigmoid()

    def forward(self, x):
        return self.sigmoid(self.linear(x))


@Language.factory("multi_label_classifier",
assigns=["doc._.multilabels"])
class MultiLabelClassifier(nn.Module):
    def __init__(self, nlp, name, n_labels):
        super().__init__()
        self.nlp = nlp
        self.model = MultiLabelModel(nlp.vocab.vectors_length,
n_labels)
        self.optimizer = optim.Adam(self.model.parameters(),
lr=0.001)
        self.loss_func = nn.BCELoss()

    def predict(self, doc: Doc) -> Doc:
        with torch.no_grad():
            vector = doc.vector
            output = self.model(torch.tensor(vector).unsqueeze(0))
            doc._.multilabels = output.squeeze().tolist()
        return doc

    def update(self, examples: list[Example], drop=0.0):
        for eg in examples:
```

```
        doc = eg.predicted
        gold = eg.reference.cats # Assuming gold labels in cats
        self.optimizer.zero_grad()
        vector = doc.vector
        prediction = self.model(torch.tensor(vector).unsqueeze(0))
                     loss  =  self.loss_func(prediction.squeeze(),
torch.tensor(list(gold.values())).float())
        loss.backward()
        self.optimizer.step()

Language.factory("multi_label_classifier",
func=MultiLabelClassifier)

# Training and usage would require a custom training loop
```

3. Data Format for Advanced Cases:

Your training data will need to reflect the hierarchical or multi-label structure. For hierarchical, you might have a single label string representing the full path in the hierarchy. For true multi-label, your annotation format needs to accommodate multiple true/false values per document.

4. Evaluation Metrics:

Standard single-label metrics like accuracy might not be appropriate. For multi-label classification, you'll often use metrics like:

Precision@k, Recall@k, F1@k (top-k predictions)

Hamming Loss

Jaccard Index

Area Under the ROC Curve (AUC) for each label

For hierarchical classification, evaluation can be more complex, considering the correctness at different levels of the hierarchy.

5. Key Considerations:

Complexity: Implementing hierarchical and true multi-label classification requires more advanced modeling techniques than standard text categorization in spaCy.

Custom Code: You'll likely need to write custom components and training loops, potentially involving external libraries like PyTorch or TensorFlow.

Data Format: Ensure your training data is correctly formatted to represent the label structure.

Evaluation: Choose appropriate evaluation metrics that reflect the nature of your classification task.

In summary, while spaCy's `TextCategorizer` handles independent multi-labeling well, hierarchical and dependent multi-label classification often necessitate building custom spaCy components with tailored model architectures and training procedures. This might involve integrating external deep learning libraries to implement the required complexity.

7.2 Leveraging spaCy for Effective Text Categorization

Leveraging spaCy for effective text categorization involves utilizing its various features and components to build accurate and efficient classification models. SpaCy provides tools for data preprocessing, feature extraction, model training, and evaluation, making it a powerful framework for this task. Here's a breakdown of how to effectively use spaCy for text categorization:

1. Data Preparation and Annotation:

Collect and Organize Data: Gather your text data and organize it into labeled categories. Ensure your dataset is representative of the texts you'll be classifying in the real world.

Annotation Format: SpaCy's `TextCategorizer` expects training data as a list of tuples, where each tuple contains the text and a dictionary of categories with boolean values (True if the category applies, False otherwise).

Python

```python
TRAIN_DATA = [
    ("This is a great movie.", {"cats": {"POSITIVE": True, "NEGATIVE": False}}),
    ("The food was terrible.", {"cats": {"POSITIVE": False, "NEGATIVE": True}}),
    ("Neutral statement here.", {"cats": {"POSITIVE": False, "NEGATIVE": False}}),
    # ... more examples
]
```

Data Splitting: Divide your data into training, validation, and test sets to properly evaluate your model's performance and prevent overfitting.

2. Choosing a Model Architecture:

SpaCy offers different architectures for text categorization, which can be configured in your `config.cfg` file:

`spacy.TextCatBOW.v2` **(Bag-of-Words):** A simple and fast architecture that uses bag-of-words features (word counts or TF-IDF) followed by a linear layer. Suitable for simpler classification tasks and as a baseline.

`spacy.TextCatCNN.v2` **(Convolutional Neural Network):** A more sophisticated architecture that uses CNNs to learn patterns in n-grams. Often performs better than BOW, especially for tasks where local word order is important.

`spacy-transformers.TextClassifier.v2`
(Transformer-based): Integrates transformer models like BERT, RoBERTa, etc., to capture rich contextual embeddings. Generally achieves state-of-the-art results but is more computationally intensive.

You select the architecture in the `[components.textcat.model.@architectures]` section of your `config.cfg`.

3. Configuring the `TextCategorizer`:

The `[components.textcat]` section in your `config.cfg` allows you to customize the behavior of the `TextCategorizer`:

`exclusive_classes`: Set to `true` for single-label classification and `false` for multi-label classification (where a text can belong to multiple categories).

`ngram_size` **(for BOW and CNN):** The size of the n-grams to consider (e.g., 1 for unigrams, 2 for bigrams).

`n_hidden` **(for CNN):** The number of hidden units in the convolutional layers.

`dropout`**:** Dropout rate for regularization.

`threshold` **(for multi-label):** The threshold above which a probability is considered a positive prediction.

4. Training the Model:

You train the text categorization model using the `spacy train` command in your terminal, providing your `config.cfg` and the paths to your training and development data in `.spacy` format.

Bash

```
python -m spacy train config.cfg --output ./output --train train.spacy --dev dev.spacy
```

SpaCy handles the training loop, optimization, and evaluation on the development set.

5. Evaluation:

After training, evaluate your model on the held-out test set using `nlp.evaluate()` or by writing a custom evaluation script. Key metrics for text categorization include:

Accuracy (for single-label): The percentage of correctly classified instances.

Precision, Recall, F1-score (per class and macro/micro averages): For both single-label and multi-label, these metrics provide a more nuanced view of the model's performance, especially on imbalanced datasets.

AUC (Area Under the ROC Curve): Useful for binary and multi-class classification.

Hamming Loss (for multi-label): The fraction of incorrectly predicted labels.

SpaCy's `Scorer` class helps calculate these metrics.

6. Iteration and Improvement:

Based on your evaluation results, iterate on your model:

Adjust Hyperparameters: Experiment with different learning rates, batch sizes, dropout rates, and architecture-specific parameters (e.g., `ngram_size`, `n_hidden`).

Feature Engineering (for BOW): While spaCy's built-in components handle feature extraction, you could preprocess your text (e.g., remove stop words, lemmatize) to potentially improve BOW performance.

Try Different Architectures: Compare the performance of BOW, CNN, and transformer-based models on your data.

Increase Training Data: More high-quality labeled data often leads to better performance. Consider data augmentation techniques.

Error Analysis: Examine misclassified examples to understand the model's weaknesses and inform your next steps.

7. Using Pre-trained Word Embeddings and Transformers:

Word Vectors: For BOW and CNN models, you can leverage pre-trained word embeddings (e.g., from spaCy's language models or other sources) to initialize the word representations. This can improve performance, especially with limited training data. Configure this in your `config.cfg`.

Transformers: As mentioned, integrating transformer models via `spacy-transformers` can significantly boost accuracy by providing rich contextual representations.

8. Deployment:

Once you have a satisfactory model, you can save it and load it for inference in your applications:

Python

```
import spacy

nlp = spacy.load("./output/model-best")
text = "This is an amazing product!"
doc = nlp(text)
print(doc.cats) # Dictionary of categories and their probabilities
```

Best Practices for Effective Text Categorization with spaCy:

Understand Your Data: Analyze the characteristics of your text data and the relationships between categories.

Choose the Right Architecture: Select a model architecture that is appropriate for the complexity of your task and the size of your dataset. Transformer models often perform best for complex tasks with sufficient data.

Proper Data Preparation: Ensure your data is clean, well-labeled, and split appropriately.

Hyperparameter Tuning: Experiment to find the optimal hyperparameters for your chosen model and data.

Rigorous Evaluation: Use appropriate metrics and a held-out test set to get an unbiased estimate of your model's performance.

Iterate and Refine: Continuously analyze your model's performance and make improvements based on your findings.

By following these steps, you can effectively leverage spaCy's capabilities to build accurate and efficient text categorization models for a wide range of applications. Remember to tailor your approach based on the specifics of your data and classification task.

7.3 Understanding and Mitigating Bias in Classification Models

Understanding and mitigating bias in classification models is a critical aspect of responsible AI development. Bias in these models can lead to unfair or discriminatory outcomes, impacting individuals and groups in negative ways. Here's a breakdown of what bias is, its sources, and strategies for mitigation, which can be applied to spaCy or any other NLP framework:

What is Bias in Classification Models?

Bias in machine learning refers to systematic errors or tendencies in a model's predictions that favor certain groups or outcomes over others. This can arise from various factors during the data collection, preprocessing, model training, and evaluation stages. A biased model doesn't generalize fairly to all parts of the population it's intended to serve.

Sources of Bias:

Data Bias:

Historical Bias: Bias present in the data reflects existing societal inequalities. If a training dataset reflects past discriminatory practices, the model may learn and perpetuate them.

Representation Bias (Sampling Bias): Occurs when the training data doesn't accurately represent the population the model will be used on. Certain groups might be over- or underrepresented.

Measurement Bias: Arises from the way data is collected and labeled. If the measurement process is flawed or inconsistent across groups, it can introduce bias.

Aggregation Bias: Occurs when models are built on aggregated data that obscures important differences between subgroups.

Reporting Bias: When the data available to train on is not representative of real-world frequencies, because some outcomes or observations are more likely to be recorded than others.

Algorithmic Bias:

Model Selection Bias: Choosing a model architecture that inherently performs better on certain types of data or for certain groups.

Optimization Bias: The training process itself might optimize for overall accuracy in a way that disadvantages minority groups.

Parameterization Bias: Choices in hyperparameters or model constraints can unintentionally favor certain groups.

User Interaction Bias: Bias introduced through user behavior or feedback that the model learns from and reinforces.

Evaluation Bias: Using evaluation metrics that don't adequately capture fairness across different groups. A model might have high overall accuracy but perform poorly on a specific subgroup.

Types of Bias:

Statistical Bias: Occurs when there are systematic differences in the data for different groups.

Cognitive Bias: Preconceived notions and stereotypes held by those involved in data collection, annotation, and model development can seep into the process.

Implicit Bias: Unconscious attitudes and stereotypes that affect our understanding, actions, and decisions.

Automation Bias: The tendency to over-rely on automated systems, assuming they are objective and free from bias.

Confirmation Bias: The tendency to interpret new evidence as confirmation of one's existing beliefs or theories.

Mitigating Bias in Classification Models:

Mitigating bias is an ongoing process that requires careful attention at every stage of the machine learning lifecycle. Here are some key strategies:

1. Data-Centric Approaches (Pre-processing):

Data Auditing and Exploration: Thoroughly analyze your data to identify potential biases in representation, distribution, and labeling across different sensitive attributes (e.g., race, gender, age).

Data Augmentation and Re-sampling:

Oversampling: Increasing the representation of underrepresented groups in the training data.

Undersampling: Decreasing the representation of overrepresented groups. Be cautious not to lose valuable information.

Synthetic Data Generation: Creating artificial data points for underrepresented groups while preserving statistical properties.

Re-weighting: Assigning different weights to training examples based on their group membership to balance the influence of different groups during training.

Data Collection Strategies: Implement strategies to collect more diverse and representative data.

2. Algorithmic Approaches (In-processing):

Fairness Constraints in Loss Functions: Modify the loss function during training to penalize models that exhibit unfair behavior across different groups. Techniques like MinDiff and Counterfactual Logit Pairing aim to balance errors or ensure similar predictions for counterfactual examples differing only by a sensitive attribute.

Adversarial Debiasing: Training an adversarial network to predict sensitive attributes from the model's learned representations. The main model is then trained to minimize prediction error while also trying to "fool" the adversary, thus removing information related to the sensitive attribute from its representations.

Fairness-Aware Algorithms: Utilize machine learning algorithms that are explicitly designed to incorporate fairness criteria during training.

Regularization Techniques: Applying regularization to prevent the model from relying too heavily on features that might be correlated with sensitive attributes.

3. Post-processing Approaches:

Threshold Adjustment: For classification tasks, adjusting the decision threshold for different groups to achieve fairness metrics like equalized odds or predictive parity.

Calibration: Ensuring that the predicted probabilities of the model are well-calibrated across different groups.

Reject Option Classification: Allowing a "reject" option for uncertain predictions, which can be useful when the model is less confident about predictions for certain groups.

4. Evaluation and Monitoring:

Use Fairness Metrics: Evaluate your models using a range of fairness metrics beyond overall accuracy, such as:

Demographic Parity: Ensuring that the proportion of positive outcomes is the same across different groups.

Equalized Odds: Ensuring that the true positive rate and false positive rate are equal across different groups.

Predictive Parity: Ensuring that the positive predictive value is equal across different groups.

Intersectionality: Consider how bias might affect individuals who belong to multiple marginalized groups.

Continuous Monitoring: Monitor the model's performance and fairness in deployment, as bias can emerge or change over time due to shifts in data distribution or societal changes.

Integrating with spaCy:

While spaCy's core library provides tools for text processing and model training, directly implementing advanced bias mitigation techniques often requires extending its functionality or integrating with other libraries, especially for algorithmic and post-processing methods.

Custom Components: You can build custom spaCy components to implement specific bias detection or mitigation steps within your pipeline.

External Libraries: Integrate with fairness-focused libraries in Python (e.g., Fairlearn, AIF360) within your training and evaluation scripts. You can extract the necessary data from spaCy Doc objects and use these libraries for bias analysis and mitigation.

Configuration: While `config.cfg` allows for setting model architectures and training parameters, more advanced fairness constraints might require custom training loops or modifications to the model architecture (potentially using libraries like PyTorch or TensorFlow if you're building custom components).

Key Considerations:

Define Fairness: Fairness is a complex and context-dependent concept. Clearly define what fairness means for your specific application and identify the relevant sensitive attributes.

Trade-offs: There often exist trade-offs between fairness and accuracy. Aim for a balance that is ethically sound and practically feasible.

Transparency and Explainability: Understand how your model makes decisions and identify potential sources of bias. Explainable AI (XAI) techniques can be valuable here.

Human Oversight: Machine learning models should not be the sole decision-makers in high-stakes applications. Human review and oversight are crucial for identifying and correcting bias.

Iterative Process: Bias mitigation is not a one-time task but an ongoing process of monitoring, evaluating, and refining your models and data.

By understanding the sources and types of bias and implementing appropriate mitigation strategies, you can strive to build more equitable and responsible classification models using spaCy and other NLP tools.

CHAPTER 8

Information Extraction Beyond Named Entities

8.1 Implementing Relation Extraction Techniques

Implementing relation extraction techniques with spaCy involves identifying relationships between entities within text. This is a crucial task for building knowledge graphs, question answering systems, and other NLP applications. Here's a breakdown of different techniques and how to approach them with spaCy:

1. Rule-Based Relation Extraction:

Rule-based systems rely on predefined patterns and linguistic rules to identify relations. These rules are typically based on dependency parses, part-of-speech tags, and regular expressions.

spaCy's `DependencyMatcher`: This tool allows you to define patterns based on the dependency tree of a sentence. You can specify the relationship between words and their syntactic roles.

Python

```
import spacy
from spacy.matcher import DependencyMatcher

nlp = spacy.load("en_core_web_sm")
matcher = DependencyMatcher(nlp.vocab)

pattern = [
```

```
  {
    "RIGHT_ID": "anchor_verb",
    "RIGHT_ATTRS": {"POS": "VERB", "LEMMA": "work"},
  },
  {
    "LEFT_ID": "anchor_verb",
    "REL": "nsubj",
    "RIGHT_ATTRS": {"POS": "NOUN", "OP": "+"},
  },
  {
    "LEFT_ID": "anchor_verb",
    "REL": "pobj",
    "RIGHT_ATTRS": {"POS": "NOUN", "OP": "+"},
  },
]

matcher.add("employee_of", [pattern])

doc = nlp("Employees work at a company.")
matches = matcher(doc)

for match_id, token_ids in matches:
    for i in token_ids:
        print(doc[i].text)
```

Custom Functions: You can write custom Python functions that analyze the spaCy Doc object and extract relations based on your own logic. This provides flexibility for complex rules.

2. Statistical Relation Extraction:

Statistical models learn to extract relations from annotated data. spaCy's built-in components are not directly designed for complex relation extraction, but you can build custom components or adapt existing ones.

Adapting `TextCategorizer`: You can potentially adapt the `TextCategorizer` to classify pairs of entities and their context into relation types. This would require creating training data where each example represents a pair of entities and their surrounding text, labeled with the relation type (or "no relation").

Custom Components with Neural Networks: For more sophisticated relation extraction, you can build custom spaCy components that incorporate neural network models (e.g., CNNs, RNNs, or Transformers). These models can learn more complex patterns and handle longer-range dependencies. You would typically use a library like PyTorch or TensorFlow within your custom component.

Relation Extraction as a Span Prediction Task: You can frame relation extraction as a span prediction task, where the model predicts the span of text that expresses the relation between two entities.

3. Transformer-Based Relation Extraction:

Transformer models, with their ability to capture contextual information, are very effective for relation extraction.

Fine-tuning Pre-trained Transformers: You can fine-tune pre-trained transformer models (e.g., BERT, RoBERTa) for relation extraction. This typically involves adding a classification layer on top of the transformer's output to predict the relation type between entity pairs.

Using `spacy-transformers`: While `spacy-transformers` doesn't provide a dedicated relation extraction component, you can build a custom component that leverages transformer embeddings. You would extract entity spans using spaCy's NER and then use the transformer embeddings for those spans (and their context) as input to a relation classification model.

Specialized Transformer Models: Explore specialized transformer models designed for relation extraction, such as those that model the relationships between entities explicitly.

4. Data Preparation and Annotation:

The performance of statistical and transformer-based relation extraction methods heavily depends on the quality and quantity of training data.

Annotation Format: You'll need to annotate your data with entities and their relationships. A common format is to represent relations as triples: (head entity, relation type, tail entity).

JSON

```
[
  {"text": "Apple was founded by Steve Jobs.", "relations": [ {"head": "Apple", "type": "founded_by", "tail": "Steve Jobs"} ]},
  {"text": "Bill Gates works at Microsoft.", "relations": [ {"head": "Bill Gates", "type": "employee_of", "tail": "Microsoft"} ]}
]
```

Tools: Use annotation tools like Doccano or Brat to annotate your data.

Data Augmentation: Consider data augmentation techniques to increase the size and diversity of your training data.

5. Evaluation:

Evaluate your relation extraction models using appropriate metrics:

Precision, Recall, F1-score: Calculate these metrics for each relation type.

Micro/Macro Averaging: Average the metrics across all relation types.

Strict vs. Relaxed Matching: Consider different matching criteria (e.g., requiring exact entity spans or allowing partial overlaps).

6. Example (Conceptual - Transformer-Based):

Python

```python
import spacy
from spacy.language import Language
from spacy.tokens import Doc
import torch
from transformers import AutoModelForSequenceClassification, AutoTokenizer

@Language.factory("transformer_relation_extractor")
class TransformerRelationExtractor:
    def __init__(self, nlp, name, model_name="bert-base-uncased", num_labels=5):
        self.tokenizer = AutoTokenizer.from_pretrained(model_name)
```

```python
                                            self.model        =
AutoModelForSequenceClassification.from_pretrained(model_nam
e, num_labels=num_labels)
        self.device = torch.device("cuda" if torch.cuda.is_available()
else "cpu")
        self.model.to(self.device)

    def __call__(self, doc: Doc) -> Doc:
        # 1. Identify entity pairs (using spaCy's NER)
        entity_pairs = []
        for ent1 in doc.ents:
            for ent2 in doc.ents:
                if ent1.start != ent2.start:
                    entity_pairs.append((ent1, ent2))

        # 2. Prepare input for the transformer (e.g., "[CLS] entity1
[SEP] relation context [SEP] entity2 [SEP]")
        relation_texts = []
        for ent1, ent2 in entity_pairs:
                        relation_context  =  doc.text[min(ent1.end,
ent2.end):max(ent1.start, ent2.start)]
            relation_text = f"[CLS] {ent1.text} [SEP] {relation_context}
[SEP] {ent2.text} [SEP]"
            relation_texts.append(relation_text)

        # 3. Tokenize and get predictions from the transformer
            inputs  =  self.tokenizer(relation_texts,  padding=True,
truncation=True, return_tensors="pt").to(self.device)
        with torch.no_grad():
            outputs = self.model(**inputs)
        predictions = torch.argmax(outputs.logits, dim=-1).tolist()

        # 4. Add relation information to the spaCy Doc (as custom
attributes)
        for (ent1, ent2), prediction in zip(entity_pairs, predictions):
```

```
        # Map prediction index to relation type (you'd need a
mapping)
        relation_type = f"REL_{prediction}"  # Example: "REL_0",
"REL_1", etc.
      if not hasattr(ent1._, "relations"):
        ent1.set_extension("relations", default=[], force=True)
        ent1._.relations.append({"target": ent2.text, "relation":
relation_type})

    return doc

Language.factory("transformer_relation_extractor",
func=TransformerRelationExtractor)

# Training and usage would require a custom training loop
```

Key Considerations:

Task Complexity: Relation extraction can be challenging, especially for complex relations or long-range dependencies.

Data Availability: Supervised methods require annotated data, which can be expensive to create.

Model Choice: Transformer models often achieve the best results but require more computational resources.

Evaluation: Use appropriate evaluation metrics to assess the performance of your relation extraction system.

By combining spaCy's text processing capabilities with rule-based systems, statistical models, or powerful transformer-based approaches, you can build effective relation extraction pipelines for your specific needs.

8.2 Building Event Extraction Pipelines with spaCy

Building event extraction pipelines with spaCy involves identifying events described in text and extracting relevant information about them, such as the trigger words, participants (arguments), time, location, and other attributes. This is a complex task that often builds upon named entity recognition (NER) and relation extraction. Here's a breakdown of techniques and how to approach them with spaCy:

1. Defining Your Event Schema:

Before building the pipeline, you need to define the types of events you're interested in and the information you want to extract for each event type. This schema might include:

Event Trigger: The word or phrase that most clearly indicates the occurrence of the event (usually a verb or a noun).

Arguments (Participants): The entities involved in the event, along with their roles (e.g., agent, patient, instrument, location, time).

Attributes: Other relevant information about the event, such as time of occurrence, location, intensity, or modality.

Example Event Schema (for a "Purchase" event):

Trigger: "bought", "purchased", "acquisition"

Buyer: The entity that performed the buying action (Agent).

Seller: The entity from whom the item was bought (Recipient/Source).

Item: The object that was bought (Patient/Theme).

Price: The amount paid (Value).

Time: When the purchase occurred.

Location: Where the purchase occurred.

2. Core Components of the Pipeline:

An event extraction pipeline with spaCy typically includes several stages:

Tokenization and Linguistic Analysis: spaCy's standard pipeline components for tokenization, POS tagging, lemmatization, and dependency parsing are essential for understanding the sentence structure and identifying potential event triggers and arguments.

Named Entity Recognition (NER): Identifying entities that can serve as arguments in events (e.g., PERSON, ORG, PRODUCT, DATE, GPE, MONEY). You'll likely need a well-performing NER model, potentially fine-tuned for your specific domain.

Event Trigger Identification: Identifying words or phrases that signal the occurrence of an event. This can be rule-based or statistical.

Argument Extraction: Identifying the entities that participate in the event and their roles. This often involves analyzing the syntactic relationships between the trigger and the entities.

Temporal and Location Extraction: Identifying temporal expressions and locations related to the event.

Relation Extraction (Event-Specific): Identifying the specific relationships between the event trigger and its arguments, assigning roles to the participants.

3. Implementation Techniques with spaCy:

a) Rule-Based Event Extraction:

Trigger Identification: Use spaCy's `Matcher` or `PhraseMatcher` to identify specific words or phrases that act as event triggers.

Argument Extraction using `DependencyMatcher`**:** Define patterns based on the dependency parse to find entities that are syntactically related to the event trigger and assign them roles based on their grammatical relations (e.g., subject as Agent, direct object as Patient, prepositional objects for location or time).

Python

```python
import spacy
from spacy.matcher import Matcher, DependencyMatcher

nlp = spacy.load("en_core_web_sm")
trigger_matcher = Matcher(nlp.vocab)
trigger_matcher.add("Purchase", [[{"LOWER": "bought"}], [{"LOWER": "purchased"}]])

dep_matcher = DependencyMatcher(nlp.vocab)
purchase_pattern = [
    {"RIGHT_ID": "trigger", "RIGHT_ATTRS": {"LEMMA": {"IN": ["buy", "purchase"]}}},
    {"LEFT_ID": "trigger", "REL": "nsubj", "OP": "?", "RIGHT_ID": "buyer"},
    {"LEFT_ID": "trigger", "REL": "dobj", "OP": "?", "RIGHT_ID": "item"},
    {"LEFT_ID": "trigger", "REL": "prep", "OP": "?", "RIGHT_ID": "prep_from"},
```

```python
        {"LEFT_ID": "prep_from", "REL": "pobj", "OP": "?", "RIGHT_ID":
"seller"},
    ]
dep_matcher.add("PurchaseArguments", [purchase_pattern])

def extract_purchase_event(doc):
    events = []
    matches = trigger_matcher(doc)
    for match_id, token_ids in matches:
        trigger = doc[token_ids[0]]
        arguments = {"Buyer": None, "Item": None, "Seller": None}
        dep_matches = dep_matcher(doc)
        for dep_match_id, dep_token_ids in dep_matches:
            if doc[dep_token_ids[0]] == trigger:
                        arg_map = {dep_token_ids[1]: "Buyer",
dep_token_ids[2]: "Item", dep_token_ids[4]: "Seller"}
                for token_index, role in arg_map.items():
                    if token_index in dep_token_ids:
                        arguments[role] = doc[token_index].text
                        events.append({"Trigger": trigger.text, "Arguments":
arguments})
    return events

doc = nlp("John bought a new car from Ford last week.")
events = extract_purchase_event(doc)
print(events)
```

Temporal and Location Extraction: Use rule-based patterns or
dedicated libraries (like `dateparser` for temporal expressions) to
identify time and location entities related to the event.

b) Statistical and Transformer-Based Event Extraction:

Adapting Existing Components: You might adapt spaCy's `TextCategorizer` to classify sentences or spans containing potential triggers and entities into event types.

Custom Neural Network Components: Build custom components with neural network architectures (CNNs, RNNs, Transformers) to jointly identify triggers and arguments. This often involves training on annotated event data.

Sequence Tagging: Frame event extraction as a sequence tagging task where each token is tagged with its role in an event (e.g., B-TRIGGER, I-TRIGGER, B-ARG-AGENT, I-ARG-AGENT, O).

Span Prediction: Use span prediction models (like those used in some question answering systems) to predict the spans of text that constitute the event trigger and its arguments.

Transformer Fine-tuning: Fine-tune pre-trained transformer models (e.g., BERT, RoBERTa) for event extraction. This typically involves adding task-specific layers on top of the transformer to predict triggers and argument roles. Libraries like `transformers` from Hugging Face provide tools for this.

c) Hybrid Approaches:

Combining rule-based and statistical methods can be effective. For example:

Use rules to identify high-confidence event triggers.

Use a statistical model to classify the roles of entities related to those triggers.

Use rules to handle specific, well-defined event types.

4. Data Annotation for Event Extraction:

Supervised statistical and transformer-based methods require annotated data. This involves marking:

Event Triggers: Identify the words that indicate events.

Event Arguments: Identify the entities participating in each event.

Argument Roles: Label the roles of each argument with respect to the trigger (e.g., Agent, Patient, Time, Location).

Event Types: Categorize each identified event into a predefined type.

Annotation tools like Doccano or specialized event annotation tools can be used for this task. The annotation process can be complex and requires clear guidelines.

5. Evaluation Metrics:

Evaluate your event extraction pipeline using metrics such as:

Precision, Recall, F1-score: Calculated for both trigger identification and argument extraction (considering both the entity and its role).

Exact Match vs. Partial Match: For arguments, you might consider partial overlaps as correct.

End-to-End Evaluation: Evaluate the entire pipeline's ability to extract complete events (trigger and all correct arguments with their roles).

6. Building the spaCy Pipeline:

Integrate your event extraction logic into a spaCy pipeline as custom components. This allows you to process text and extract events in a structured way.

Python

```
nlp = spacy.load("en_core_web_sm")
nlp.add_pipe("my_event_extractor",          last=True)          #
"my_event_extractor" would be your custom component
doc = nlp("The company acquired a startup for $10 million last
year.")
for event in doc._.events: # Access extracted events from the Doc
object
    print(event)
```

Key Considerations:

Domain Specificity: Event extraction is often highly domain-specific. The types of events and their arguments will vary greatly depending on the domain.

Complexity of Language: Natural language is complex, and events can be expressed in many different ways.

Annotation Effort: Creating high-quality annotated data for supervised methods is time-consuming and requires expertise.

Handling Implicit Arguments: Sometimes, event arguments are not explicitly mentioned but are implied by the context.

Coreference Resolution: Resolving coreferences (e.g., pronouns referring to entities) can be crucial for identifying all participants in an event.

Building an effective event extraction pipeline with spaCy requires a careful combination of linguistic understanding, rule design (if using rule-based methods), machine learning techniques (if using statistical or transformer-based methods), and a well-defined event schema. The choice of approach will depend on the complexity of the events you want to extract, the amount of annotated data available, and the desired level of accuracy.

8.3 Extracting Complex Information Structures

Extracting complex information structures with spaCy goes beyond simple named entity recognition and relation extraction. It involves identifying intricate relationships, nested entities, events with multiple arguments, and potentially representing this information in a structured format like JSON, RDF triples, or custom graph-like objects. Here's a breakdown of techniques and strategies to achieve this with spaCy:

1. Defining Your Target Information Structure:

Before you start, clearly define the complex information you want to extract. This includes:

Entity Types: Including nested or granular entity types (e.g., a `PRODUCT` might have sub-entities like `MODEL_NUMBER`, `MANUFACTURER`).

Relationship Types: Defining a richer set of relationships, possibly with attributes (e.g., a `PURCHASE` relation might have a `QUANTITY` and `PRICE`).

Event Structures: Specifying the types of events you're interested in, their triggers, participants (with roles), and attributes (time, location, etc.).

Discourse Structures: Identifying relationships that span across sentences or paragraphs (e.g., causal relations, temporal sequences).

2. Layered and Nested Entity Recognition:

Multiple NER Passes: Run multiple NER models in sequence. The output of one model can provide context for the next. For example, first identify broad entity types, then a second model can identify subtypes within those entities.

Custom NER Architectures: Build or adapt NER models to predict nested entities directly. This might involve modifying the output layer to predict spans and their nesting levels. Libraries like `torch-struct` could be helpful for structured prediction.

Rule-Based Refinement: Use `Matcher` or custom functions based on dependency parses to identify and annotate nested entities based on syntactic patterns around already identified entities.

3. Advanced Relation Extraction:

N-ary Relations: Extract relationships involving more than two entities. This might require identifying a central "anchor" word (often a verb or a noun) and then finding its related entities through dependency parsing.

Relation Attributes: Extend relation extraction to capture attributes of the relationship itself. This could involve classifying the relation and simultaneously extracting related information (e.g., extracting a PURCHASE relation and also the DATE and PRICE associated with it).

Contextual Relation Extraction: Use the broader context of the sentence or document to improve relation extraction accuracy, especially for ambiguous cases. Transformer models excel at this.

Graph-Based Approaches: Represent the entities and their potential relations as a graph and use graph neural networks (GNNs) or graph traversal algorithms to infer complex relationships.

4. Event Extraction with Argument Roles and Attributes:

Trigger Identification: Use rule-based or statistical methods to identify event trigger words.

Argument Role Labeling: Classify the roles of entities with respect to the event trigger. This can be framed as a sequence labeling or a dependency parsing subtask.

Attribute Extraction: Identify and link attributes (time, location, modality) to the extracted events and their arguments.

Coreference Resolution: Resolve pronouns and other coreferring expressions to ensure all participants in an event are correctly identified, even if mentioned using different phrases.

5. Discourse-Level Information Extraction:

Connective Identification: Identify discourse connectives (e.g., "because," "however," "then") that signal relationships between clauses or sentences.

Discourse Relation Classification: Classify the type of discourse relation (e.g., causality, contrast, temporal sequence).

Argument Identification for Discourse Relations: Determine which spans of text are connected by the identified discourse relations.

6. Representing Complex Information Structures:

Once extracted, you need a way to represent these structures:

JSON: A flexible format for representing nested objects and lists, suitable for many complex structures.

RDF Triples (Subject-Predicate-Object): Useful for building knowledge graphs where entities are nodes and relations are edges. You might need to decompose complex structures into sets of triples.

Custom Graph Objects: Create Python classes to represent entities, relations, and events as nodes and edges in a graph, allowing for more complex relationships and traversals.

7. Implementing with spaCy (and potentially other libraries):

Custom Pipeline Components: The core of your implementation will likely involve building several custom spaCy pipeline components for each stage of the extraction process (e.g., a more sophisticated NER, a relation extractor with attribute handling, an event argument role labeler).

Rule-Based Components (`Matcher`, `DependencyMatcher`): Use these for pattern-based extraction of specific structures or for refining the output of statistical models.

Statistical Models (Custom Training): Train custom statistical models (potentially using libraries like scikit-learn or a deep learning framework integrated with spaCy) for tasks like relation attribute classification or event argument role labeling.

Transformer Models (`spacy-transformers`): Leverage transformer models for their strong contextual understanding, especially for complex relation extraction and event extraction tasks. You might fine-tune a transformer for a specific subtask (e.g., classifying the role of an entity in an event).

Integration with External Libraries: For tasks like coreference resolution (e.g., `neuralcoref`, `spaCy-alias`), temporal expression parsing (e.g., `dateparser`), or building knowledge graphs (e.g., `rdflib`), you'll likely need to integrate external libraries within your custom spaCy components.

Data Annotation: High-quality, structured annotations are crucial for training statistical models for complex information extraction. You'll need to annotate not just entities and relations, but also roles, attributes, and potentially event structures.

Example (Conceptual Custom Component for Relation with Attributes):

Python

```python
import spacy
from spacy.language import Language
from spacy.tokens import Doc, Span

@Language.factory("relation_attribute_extractor",
assigns=["doc._.complex_relations"])
class RelationAttributeExtractor:
    def __init__(self, nlp, name):
        # Load a pre-trained model or initialize your model
        pass

    def __call__(self, doc: Doc) -> Doc:
        relations = []
```

```python
    for token in doc:
        if token.dep_ == "ROOT" and token.pos_ == "VERB":
            # Look for subjects and objects
            subject = [t for t in token.subtree if t.dep_ == "nsubj" and
t.ent_type_]
                object_ = [t for t in token.subtree if t.dep_ in ["dobj",
"pobj"] and t.ent_type_]
            if subject and object_:
                    relation = {"subject": subject[0].text, "object":
object_[0].text, "type": token.lemma_}
                    # Try to find attributes of the relation (e.g., using
dependency parsing)
                for child in token.children:
                    if child.dep_ == "prep" and child.lemma_ == "for":
                        amount = [c for c in child.children if c.ent_type_
== "MONEY"]
                    if amount:
                        relation["price"] = amount[0].text
                relations.append(relation)
        doc._.complex_relations = relations
        return doc


Language.factory("relation_attribute_extractor",
func=RelationAttributeExtractor)

nlp = spacy.load("en_core_web_sm")
nlp.add_pipe("relation_attribute_extractor")
doc = nlp("Apple acquired a startup for $1 billion in 2023.")
print(doc._.complex_relations)
```

Key Challenges:

Annotation Complexity: Annotating complex structures is more difficult and time-consuming than simple NER or relation annotation.

Model Complexity: Building models that can accurately extract these structures often requires more sophisticated architectures and training strategies.

Evaluation: Defining appropriate evaluation metrics for complex information structures can be challenging.

Integration: Combining different techniques and libraries within a cohesive spaCy pipeline requires careful design and implementation.

Extracting complex information structures with spaCy is an advanced NLP task that often requires a combination of rule-based and statistical methods, potentially leveraging the power of transformer models and integrating with external libraries. The key is to have a clear definition of your target information structure and to build a pipeline of custom components that work together to identify and represent this information effectively.

CHAPTER 9

Deploying spaCy Models in Production Environments

9.1 Containerizing spaCy Applications with Docker

Containerizing spaCy applications with Docker is a best practice for ensuring consistent and reproducible deployments across different environments. Docker packages your application and its dependencies into a self-contained unit called a container, making it easy to run anywhere Docker is installed. Here's a comprehensive guide on how to containerize your spaCy applications:

1. Create a `Dockerfile`:

The `Dockerfile` is a text file that contains instructions for building your Docker image. Create a file named `Dockerfile` in the root directory of your spaCy application.

```
Dockerfile

# Use an official Python runtime as a parent image
FROM python:3.9-slim-buster

# Set the working directory in the container
WORKDIR /app

# Copy the application code and requirements file to the container
COPY requirements.txt .
COPY . .
```

```
# Install any dependencies
RUN pip install --no-cache-dir -r requirements.txt

# Download spaCy language models (adjust as needed)
RUN python -m spacy download en_core_web_sm
RUN python -m spacy download de_core_news_sm

# Expose any necessary ports (if your application is a web service)
# EXPOSE 8000

# Define the command to run your application
CMD ["python", "main.py"]
```

Explanation of the `Dockerfile`:

`FROM python:3.9-slim-buster`: Specifies the base image to use, which is an official lightweight Python 3.9 image based on Debian Buster. Choose a Python version compatible with your application.

`WORKDIR /app`: Sets the working directory inside the container to `/app`. Subsequent commands will be executed in this directory.

`COPY requirements.txt .` **and** `COPY . .`: Copies the `requirements.txt` file (listing your Python dependencies) and all other files from your application directory on your host machine to the `/app` directory in the container.

`RUN pip install --no-cache-dir -r requirements.txt`: Installs the Python dependencies listed in `requirements.txt` inside the container. The `--no-cache-dir` flag prevents pip from using the cache, ensuring a clean installation.

`RUN python -m spacy download en_core_web_sm` **and** `RUN python -m spacy download de_core_news_sm`: Downloads the necessary spaCy language models directly into the container during the image build process. Adjust the model names based on the languages your application uses.

`EXPOSE 8000` **(Optional):** If your spaCy application is a web service (e.g., using Flask or FastAPI), specify the port it will listen on.

`CMD ["python", "main.py"]`: Defines the default command to run when the container starts. Replace `main.py` with the entry point of your spaCy application.

2. Create a `requirements.txt` **File:**

List all the Python dependencies your spaCy application needs in a file named `requirements.txt` in the root directory of your project. This should include `spacy` and any other libraries you are using (e.g., Flask, FastAPI, pandas, scikit-learn, `spacy-transformers`).

```
spacy
en_core_web_sm
de_core_news_sm
fastapi
uvicorn
# Add other dependencies here
```

3. Build the Docker Image:

Open your terminal, navigate to the root directory of your spaCy application (where the `Dockerfile` and `requirements.txt` are located), and run the following command to build the Docker image:

Bash

docker build -t spacy-app .

`docker build`: The command to build a Docker image.

`-t spacy-app`: Tags the image with the name `spacy-app`. You can choose any name you like.

`.`: Specifies the build context, which is the current directory. Docker will use files in this directory during the build process.

Docker will download the base image, execute the instructions in the `Dockerfile`, and create a Docker image named `spacy-app`.

4. Run the Docker Container:

Once the image is built successfully, you can run a container from it using the `docker run` command:

Bash

docker run -p 8000:8000 spacy-app

`docker run`: The command to run a Docker container.

`-p 8000:8000` **(Optional):** If your application exposes a port (e.g., 8000), this maps port 8000 on your host machine to port 8000 inside the container. Adjust the port numbers as needed.

`spacy-app`: The name of the Docker image you built.

Your spaCy application should now be running inside the Docker container. You can access it through the specified port on your host machine if it's a web service.

5. Optimizations and Best Practices:

Multi-Stage Builds: For more complex applications, consider using multi-stage builds in your `Dockerfile` to reduce the final image size. This involves using separate build stages for installing dependencies and then copying only the necessary artifacts to a smaller runtime image.

Environment Variables: Use environment variables to configure your application within the container instead of hardcoding values in your code. You can set environment variables using the `-e` flag with `docker run` or in a `docker-compose.yml` file.

`.dockerignore` **File:** Create a `.dockerignore` file in the root directory to exclude unnecessary files and directories (e.g., `.git`, `__pycache__`, virtual environment folders) from being copied into the Docker image, reducing its size and build time.

Specific Base Images: Choose base images that are as minimal as possible while still meeting your application's requirements. Slim versions of Python images are often a good choice.

Health Checks: If your application is a service, define health checks in your `Dockerfile` or `docker-compose.yml` so that Docker can monitor the health of your containers.

Logging: Configure your application to log appropriately, and consider using Docker logging drivers to manage container logs.

Orchestration: For more complex deployments involving multiple containers, consider using Docker Compose or a container orchestration platform like Kubernetes.

Example `.dockerignore` **File:**

```
.git
__pycache__
venv
*.pyc
*.log
data/ # If you don't need your local data in the image
```

Using Docker Compose (for multi-container applications):

If your spaCy application relies on other services (e.g., a database), you can use Docker Compose to define and manage multiple containers. Create a `docker-compose.yml` file in your project root:

YAML

```yaml
version: '3.8'
services:
  web:
    build: .
    ports:
      - "8000:8000"
    volumes:
      - .:/app
    depends_on:
      # - database
    environment:
      # - DATABASE_URL=...
    command: ["python", "main.py"]
```

```
# database:
#   image: postgres:13
#   environment:
#     - POSTGRES_USER=...
#     - POSTGRES_PASSWORD=...
```

Then, you can start your application and its dependencies with:

Bash

```
docker-compose up -d
```

Containerizing your spaCy applications with Docker provides numerous benefits for deployment, scalability, and reproducibility. By following these steps and best practices, you can ensure that your applications run consistently across different environments.

9.2 Serving spaCy Models with REST APIs

Imagine your amazing spaCy model as a **specialized text analysis robot** that lives inside your computer. This robot is super good at understanding language – it can pick out names, places, and organizations, figure out what words mean, and even understand how words relate to each other in a sentence.

Now, you want to let other computer programs or apps that are running *outside* your computer (maybe on someone else's computer or on a website) use this smart robot. They can't just directly access the robot inside your machine.

So, you build a **special delivery window** for your robot. This delivery window is called a **REST API**.

Here's how it works:

1.The Outside Program (The Customer): This program has some text it wants your spaCy robot to analyze. It packages this text into a **request** – like placing an order at the delivery window.

2. The Delivery Window (The REST API): This window has a specific address (a URL) and accepts specific kinds of "orders" (like "process this text"). You build this window using tools like Flask or FastAPI – they are like the framework for your delivery service.

3. The Messenger (The Web Framework): When an "order" (request) arrives at the delivery window, Flask or FastAPI (the messenger) takes the text and passes it to your spaCy robot inside.

4. The Smart Robot (Your spaCy Model): Your spaCy model gets the text and does its magic – it analyzes it according to how you trained it.

5. Preparing the Delivery (Processing the Results): The spaCy model produces the analyzed information – maybe a list of all the people and places it found, or the grammatical structure of the sentence.

6. Packaging the Delivery (Formatting the Response): Flask or FastAPI takes this analyzed information and packages it into a standard format that the outside program can easily understand, usually as a **JSON package** (think of a neatly labeled box).

7. Sending the Delivery Back (The API Response): The messenger sends this JSON package back to the outside program through the delivery window.

8. The Outside Program Gets the Analysis: The program receives the JSON package and can now use the information that your smart spaCy robot provided.

So, serving your spaCy model with a REST API is like creating a way for other programs to send text to your smart language robot over the internet and get back the analyzed results in a structured and easy-to-use format, without needing to know anything about how the robot actually works inside.

9.3 Monitoring and Maintaining Deployed NLP Systems

Monitoring and maintaining deployed NLP systems is crucial for ensuring their reliability, performance, and fairness over time. Unlike static software, NLP models can degrade due to data drift, concept drift, changes in user behavior, and the emergence of new patterns in language. A proactive approach to monitoring and maintenance helps identify and address these issues before they significantly impact the system's effectiveness.

Here's a breakdown of key aspects of monitoring and maintaining deployed NLP systems:

1. Defining Key Performance Indicators (KPIs) and Metrics:

Business KPIs: Align your monitoring efforts with the business goals the NLP system supports. For example, if it's a customer service chatbot, KPIs might include resolution rate, customer satisfaction scores, and task completion time.

Model Performance Metrics: Track the traditional NLP evaluation metrics relevant to your task (e.g., accuracy, precision, recall, F1-score for classification and information extraction; BLEU, ROUGE for text generation).

Latency and Throughput: Monitor the time it takes for the system to process requests and the number of requests it can handle within a given time frame. This is crucial for user experience and scalability.

Resource Utilization: Track CPU usage, memory consumption, and disk I/O of the deployed system to identify potential bottlenecks or resource exhaustion.

Cost Metrics: If applicable, monitor the cost associated with running the NLP system (e.g., cloud compute costs, API usage).

2. Implementing Monitoring Infrastructure:

Logging: Implement comprehensive logging to record requests, responses, errors, and intermediate processing steps. Structured logging (e.g., using JSON format) makes it easier to analyze logs.

Metrics Collection: Use monitoring tools and libraries to collect and store the defined KPIs and metrics. Options include Prometheus, Grafana, Datadog, and cloud-specific monitoring services (e.g., AWS CloudWatch, Azure Monitor, Google Cloud Monitoring).

Alerting: Set up alerts based on thresholds for critical metrics. For example, trigger an alert if latency exceeds a certain limit, error rates spike, or performance metrics drop significantly.

Visualization: Use dashboards (e.g., in Grafana, Kibana) to visualize trends in your metrics, making it easier to identify anomalies and patterns.

Tracing: For complex NLP systems with multiple components, implement distributed tracing to understand the flow of requests and pinpoint the source of performance issues.

3. Monitoring for Data and Concept Drift:

Data Drift: Monitor the input data distribution over time to detect significant changes. This can involve tracking statistics of input features (e.g., word frequencies, sentence lengths, entity distributions). Tools like Evidently AI, Fiddler AI, and MLflow provide data drift detection capabilities.

Concept Drift: Monitor the relationship between input features and the target variable (or the desired output) to detect changes. This is harder to detect directly but can be inferred from drops in model performance or changes in error patterns.

Monitoring Input Quality: Track metrics related to the quality of the input data (e.g., percentage of malformed requests, unexpected characters).

4. Monitoring Model Performance in Production:

Shadow Deployment (A/B Testing): Deploy new model versions alongside the existing one and route a small percentage of live traffic to the new model. Compare their performance on real-world data before fully rolling out the new version.

Canary Releases: Gradually roll out a new model version to an increasing percentage of users while continuously monitoring its performance and error rates.

Feedback Loops: Implement mechanisms for users to provide feedback on the system's outputs. This feedback can be valuable for identifying issues and areas for improvement.

Human-in-the-Loop (HITL): For critical applications, have human reviewers examine a sample of the system's outputs to identify errors or biases that automated metrics might miss.

5. Maintaining and Updating Deployed Models:

Retraining: Regularly retrain your models with new data to account for data and concept drift. Automate this process as much as possible.

Fine-tuning: Fine-tune existing models on new, relevant data instead of retraining from scratch, which can be more efficient.

Model Versioning: Keep track of different model versions and the data and configurations used to train them. This allows for easy rollback if a new version performs poorly.

Regular Evaluation: Continuously evaluate the performance of the deployed model on a representative evaluation dataset.

Addressing Bias: Monitor for and mitigate bias in the deployed system. This might involve retraining with debiased data or applying post-processing techniques.

Updating Dependencies: Regularly update the underlying libraries and frameworks (e.g., spaCy, transformers, web frameworks) to benefit from bug fixes, security patches, and performance improvements.

Security Audits: Conduct regular security audits of your deployed NLP system to identify and address potential vulnerabilities.

6. Infrastructure Maintenance:

Scaling: Monitor resource utilization and scale the infrastructure (e.g., number of servers, container instances) as needed to handle changes in traffic.

Load Balancing: Distribute incoming traffic across multiple instances of your application to ensure high availability and prevent overload.

Disaster Recovery: Have a plan in place for recovering from failures or outages.

Cost Optimization: Continuously review resource usage and identify opportunities to optimize costs.

7. Tools and Technologies:

Monitoring Platforms: Prometheus, Grafana, Datadog, Kibana, cloud-specific monitoring services.

MLOps Platforms: MLflow, Kubeflow, SageMaker MLOps, Azure Machine Learning MLOps.

Data and Concept Drift Detection Libraries: Evidently AI, Fiddler AI, NannyML.

Logging Libraries: Python's built-in `logging` module, structured logging libraries like `structlog`.

Tracing Tools: Jaeger, Zipkin.

Containerization: Docker, Kubernetes.

Applying to spaCy Systems:

When deploying NLP systems built with spaCy, the principles above still apply. You'll monitor the performance of your spaCy pipelines (e.g., NER accuracy, parsing speed), the resource utilization of your API servers, and look for signs of drift in the text data being processed. Maintenance might involve retraining your spaCy models with new annotated data or fine-tuning transformer-based components. Containerization with Docker (as discussed previously) simplifies deployment and ensures consistent environments for your spaCy applications.

Effective monitoring and maintenance are not afterthoughts but integral parts of the NLP system development lifecycle. By proactively addressing potential issues, you can ensure that your deployed NLP systems remain reliable, performant, and provide value over time.

CHAPTER 10

The Future of spaCy and Advanced NLP Trends

10.1 Exploring Emerging Trends in Natural Language Processing

emerging trends in Natural Language Processing (NLP), as of late 2024 and looking into 2025. Here's a breakdown of the key areas gaining momentum:

1. The Dominance and Advancement of Large Language Models (LLMs):

Models like **GPT-4**, **BERT**, **T5**, **PaLM 2**, and **XLM-R** continue to be central. They're improving in language understanding and generation with unprecedented accuracy.[1]

Fine-tuning LLMs for specific tasks (chatbots, summarization, content generation) is a major focus.[2]

Scalability is improving, allowing these models to handle larger datasets more efficiently.[3]

There's a push for **broader accessibility** of advanced LLM technologies for various businesses.

We're seeing **more specialization** of models for particular industries and tasks.

2. Multimodal NLP:

This involves combining NLP with other AI technologies like **computer vision** and **speech recognition**.[4]

The goal is for AI systems to understand and interact with the world more robustly by analyzing both visual and textual data (and potentially audio).[5]

This leads to more capable virtual assistants and other applications.[6]

3. Multilingual NLP:

Developing models capable of processing and understanding **multiple languages simultaneously** is crucial for breaking down communication barriers.[7]

Models like **mBERT** (Multilingual BERT) and **XLM-R** are designed for cross-lingual understanding.[8]

Applications include localized customer support, sentiment analysis across languages, and automatic translation.[9]

4. Enhanced Understanding and Generation:

Advanced Context Understanding: NLP models are getting better at grasping nuances, implied meanings, and user intent.[10]

Real-Time Information Synthesis: The ability to quickly process and summarize information in real-time is improving.[11]

Conversational Continuity: Chatbots and virtual assistants are becoming better at maintaining coherent and engaging conversations.[12]

Enhanced Creative Writing Support: NLP tools are assisting with drafting emails, messages, and even more creative content, matching tone and style.[13]

5. Focus on Ethical AI:

There's a growing emphasis on **fairness and inclusivity** in NLP systems to serve all users equitably.[14]

Transparency in AI models is gaining importance, with efforts to make decision-making processes more understandable and accountable.[15]

Developing ethical frameworks for implementing reinforcement learning responsibly is also a trend.

6. Real-Time Applications:

Real-time language translation is becoming increasingly accurate, enhancing global communication for customer support, meetings, and personal interactions.[16]

Advancements in speech recognition are contributing to more seamless real-time communication.[17]

7. Integration and Accessibility:

Tools like **LangChain** are facilitating the use of multiple AI and LLM technologies to solve complex problems (combinatorial AI).[18]

There's a trend toward **low-code/no-code NLP tools**, making the technology more accessible to a wider range of users and businesses.

In essence, the field of NLP is rapidly advancing, driven by the power of large language models, the need for more human-like interaction with technology, and a growing awareness of ethical considerations.[19] These trends are shaping the future of how we interact with machines and how machines understand and process the vast amounts of human language data available.

10.2 Understanding spaCy's Roadmap and Potential Developments

The official spaCy roadmap isn't a fixed, publicly detailed document with specific timelines for major releases like "spaCy 4.0". However, we can understand the potential developments and future direction of spaCy by looking at:

Past Releases and Trends: Analyzing the features and improvements in recent versions (especially the significant shift introduced with spaCy 3.0 and its focus on transformers and the projects system) gives clues about future directions.

The spaCy Universe: The ecosystem of extensions, plugins, and integrations developed by the community highlights areas of interest and potential official adoption.

Emerging Trends in NLP: SpaCy aims to be a cutting-edge library, so it will likely incorporate advancements in the broader NLP field.

Discussions and Issues on GitHub: While not a formal roadmap, the issues and discussions on the spaCy GitHub repository can indicate areas the developers are actively working on or considering.

Blog Posts and Announcements from Explosion (the company behind spaCy): These often provide insights into the team's current focus and future plans.

Based on these factors, here are potential developments and trends to watch for in spaCy's future:

Likely Continued Development Areas:

Enhanced Large Language Model (LLM) Integration: Following the introduction of the `spacy-llm` package, we can expect deeper and more seamless integration of LLMs into spaCy pipelines. This might involve better ways to prompt LLMs, structure their output, and combine them with traditional spaCy components.

Improved Transformer Support: Expect continued updates and improvements to the `spacy-transformers` library, potentially incorporating new transformer architectures and optimization techniques.

More Robust and User-Friendly Training Features: Building on the v3.0 configuration system and the projects system, spaCy will likely continue to refine its training workflows, making it easier to train custom models with more control and reproducibility.

Expansion of Language Support and Resources: The addition of new language models and improvements to existing language data are ongoing efforts. We might see more community-contributed language packs and enhanced multilingual capabilities.

Focus on Efficiency and Scalability: SpaCy has always been known for its speed. Future developments will likely continue to prioritize performance optimizations, especially for large-scale NLP tasks.

Strengthening the spaCy Projects System: The projects system, introduced in v3.0, provides end-to-end workflows. Expect enhancements to this system, making it even easier to manage data preprocessing, training, evaluation, and deployment.

Further Development of the Ecosystem: The "spaCy Universe" of external tools and libraries is a valuable asset. We might see closer integration or official support for some of these key extensions.

Improved Tools for Data Annotation: While Prodigy is a separate paid tool from Explosion, there might be more open-source initiatives or better integration with annotation workflows to streamline data creation for spaCy models.

Emphasis on Responsible AI: As the NLP field increasingly focuses on ethical considerations, spaCy might incorporate more tools or best practices for detecting and mitigating bias in language models.

Potential "SpaCy 4.0" Directions (Hypothetical):

While a specific "spaCy 4.0" isn't formally announced, a major version release could potentially involve:

Significant Architectural Changes: While v3.0 brought a major shift, a v4.0 could introduce even more fundamental changes to the library's core structure or API, although this is less likely in the short term given the stability of v3.x.

First-Class Support for New Modalities: Deeper integration of audio or visual processing directly within spaCy's core framework, moving beyond just text. This would be a significant undertaking.

More Native Deep Learning Framework Integration: While spaCy already works with PyTorch and TensorFlow through Thinc, a major version might see even tighter, more streamlined integration.

Rethinking Core Data Structures: Potential evolution of the Doc object or other fundamental data structures to better accommodate new NLP paradigms.

Staying Updated:

The best ways to stay informed about spaCy's roadmap and potential developments are to:

Follow the official spaCy blog: This is where major announcements and insights are typically shared.

Monitor the spaCy GitHub repository: Keep an eye on releases, issues, and pull requests.

Engage with the spaCy community: Participate in discussions on forums and social media.

Attend talks and presentations by the spaCy core team: These often provide glimpses into future plans.

In conclusion, while a formal roadmap with version numbers and specific features isn't publicly available, the trajectory of spaCy points towards continued advancements in LLM integration, transformer support, training workflows, language coverage, performance, and the overall ecosystem, with a growing awareness of responsible AI practices. A hypothetical "spaCy 4.0" could potentially involve more significant architectural changes or the integration of new modalities, but the evolution is more likely to be incremental within the v3.x series for the near future.

10.3 Contributing to the spaCy Ecosystem and Community

Contributing to the spaCy ecosystem and community is a fantastic way to help advance the field of NLP, learn from others, and make a real impact. There are many ways to get involved, regardless of your experience level. Here's a breakdown of how you can contribute:

1. Code Contributions:

Bug Fixes: Identify and fix bugs in the core library or its extensions. Check the spaCy GitHub repository for open issues labeled "bug".

New Features: Propose and implement new features or enhancements to spaCy's core functionality, language models, or training pipelines. Discuss your ideas on GitHub issues or the discussion forum before starting significant work.

Language Data and Models: Contribute to the development of language-specific data, such as lemmatization tables, stop word lists, or even train new language models (especially for under-resourced languages).

Integration with Other Libraries: Develop or improve integrations with other relevant NLP or data science libraries.

Performance Improvements: Identify and implement optimizations to improve spaCy's speed and efficiency.

Typing and Documentation: Improve type hints or add/enhance docstrings and documentation.

How to Contribute Code:

1.Find an Issue: Look for open issues on the spaCy GitHub repository that you're interested in working on. Start with issues labeled "good first issue" if you're new to contributing.

2. Fork the Repository: Create your own copy (fork) of the `explosion/spaCy` repository on GitHub.

3. Create a Branch: Create a new branch in your fork for your changes (e.g., `fix-bug-123`, `add-new-feature`).

4. Make Your Changes: Write your code, following spaCy's coding style and contributing guidelines. Include tests for your changes.

5. Commit Your Changes: Commit your changes with clear and concise commit messages.

6. Push to Your Fork: Push your branch to your GitHub fork.

7. Create a Pull Request (PR): On the original `explosion/spaCy` repository, create a new pull request from your branch. Clearly describe the changes you've made and reference the issue you're addressing (if any).

8. Code Review: Your pull request will be reviewed by the spaCy core team. Be prepared to make revisions based on their feedback.

9. Merge: Once the review is successful, your changes will be merged into the main spaCy repository.

2. Documentation Contributions:

Improving Existing Documentation: Clarify ambiguous explanations, fix typos, add more examples, or improve the overall structure and readability of the documentation.

Translating Documentation: Help translate spaCy's documentation into other languages.

Creating Tutorials and Examples: Write blog posts, tutorials, or create example scripts that demonstrate how to use spaCy for specific tasks.

How to Contribute to Documentation:

1.Find Areas for Improvement: Identify sections of the documentation that are unclear, incomplete, or could be enhanced.

2. Fork the `explosion/spaCy-docs` **repository:** Create your own fork of the documentation repository.

3. Make Your Changes: Edit the documentation files (usually written in Markdown or reStructuredText).

4. Build the Documentation (Locally): Follow the instructions in the documentation repository to build it locally and preview your changes.

5. Commit and Push: Commit your changes and push them to your fork.

6. Create a Pull Request: Create a pull request to the `explosion/spaCy-docs` repository, describing your changes.

3. Community Engagement and Support:

Answering Questions: Help other users on the spaCy Discussions forum, Stack Overflow (with the `spacy` tag), or other community channels.

Sharing Your Projects and Use Cases: Write blog posts, share code snippets, or present at meetups and conferences about how you're using spaCy.

Reporting Issues: If you encounter bugs or unexpected behavior, create detailed and reproducible bug reports on the spaCy GitHub repository. This is incredibly valuable for the core team.

Participating in Discussions: Engage in discussions on GitHub issues and the forum, sharing your ideas and perspectives.

Organizing or Speaking at Events: Organize local spaCy meetups or workshops, or volunteer to speak about your spaCy projects.

4. Contributing to the spaCy Universe:

Developing and Maintaining Extensions: Create and share useful spaCy extensions (e.g., for specific tasks, integrations with other tools, or new model architectures). Consider publishing them in the "spaCy Universe" on the spaCy website.

Creating Language Resources: Develop and share language-specific resources like rule-based matchers, lexical data, or pre-trained word vectors.

5. Financial Contributions:

Sponsoring spaCy Development: If you or your organization benefits significantly from spaCy, consider financially supporting its development through platforms like GitHub Sponsors. This helps ensure the project's long-term sustainability.

Tips for Effective Contributions:

Read the Contributing Guidelines: Familiarize yourself with spaCy's specific contributing guidelines on GitHub. This will help ensure your contributions are aligned with the project's standards.

Start Small: If you're new to contributing, begin with smaller tasks like bug fixes or documentation improvements to get familiar with the workflow.

Communicate: Clearly communicate your intentions and progress on GitHub issues or the forum.

Be Patient and Respectful: Code review and merging take time. Be patient and respectful of the core team's feedback.

Write Tests: Ensure your code contributions include adequate tests to verify their correctness.

Follow Coding Style: Adhere to spaCy's coding style conventions.

By contributing in any of these ways, you become a vital part of the spaCy ecosystem, helping to make this powerful NLP library even better for everyone. Your contributions, big or small, are highly valued!